BUMPER INSTANT ART
for
Advent and Christmas

Kathryn Atkins

kevin
mayhew

kevin
mayhew

First published in Great Britain in 1999 by Kevin Mayhew Ltd
Buxhall, Stowmarket, Suffolk IP14 3BW
Tel: +44 (0) 1449 737978 Fax: +44 (0) 1449 737834
E-mail: info@kevinmayhewltd.com

www.kevinmayhew.com

© Copyright 1999 Kevin Mayhew.

The right of Kevin Mayhew to be identified as the author of this work
has been asserted by him in accordance with the Copyright, Designs
and Patents Act 1988.

All rights reserved. No part of this publication may be reproduced,
stored in a retrieval system, or transmitted, in any form or by any
means, electronic, mechanical, photocopying, recording, or otherwise,
without the prior written permission of the publisher.

9 8 7 6 5 4 3 2 0D

ISBN 978 1 84003 443 1
Catalogue No. 1396069

Cover design by Jaquetta Sergeant
Typeset by Elisabeth Bates

Printed and bound in Great Britain

Introduction

Make Advent and Christmas extra special and exciting with this magnificent book of creative projects. This collection has something for children of all ages and can be used in many situations: day schools, mid-week clubs, family services, Sunday schools, nurseries, playgroups or at home.

• copyright

Material in this book is copyright-free, provided that it is used for the purposes for which it is intended. (Reproduction of the contents of this book for commercial purposes is subject to the usual copyright restrictions.)

• suggestions for use

For some of the activities you may want to tell the story in some way, e.g. drama, storytelling, overhead projector drawing. Other activities could be used for more extended craft sessions through Advent – for example, the Christmas Alphabet frieze which consists of seven pages to be coloured in.

You will need to make one photocopy for each child – unless you are working together on a group project, for example, assembling the crib scene. Most of the activities would be better on card but some only need paper. Always encourage the children to colour in parts of any model *before* assembling it.

• photocopying onto card

Most photocopiers will take a fine grade of card, and photocopying models straight onto card rather than gluing a paper copy to card achieves a much better and quicker result.

Fine card (A4 size) suitable for photocopying should be available in large packs from suppliers of photocopy paper or from printers. The card will probably need to be *hand fed* into the photocopier, but this does not take too long.

• equipment required

It is a good idea to make up one model yourself at home at first – this gives you a knowledge of the steps to follow and the equipment you will need, and gives the children a visual demonstration of the finished model.

Good Scissors – an essential, but should have round points.

Colouring Pens – cheap packs of felt tip pens are readily available.

Crayons – better for young children for some of the activities.

Glue – solid stick glue with a twist-up end is best. It is quite expensive, but holds in place well for small tabs, etc, and is not too messy.

Paper Fasteners – available from stationers in boxes of 100 (size 15mm is a useful size).

Sharp point – compasses are useful to pierce holes before inserting paper fasteners. NB *piercing holes only to be done by an adult for safety.*

Stapler – invest in a heavy-duty stapler.

Craft knife – only to be used by an adult for safety. This is useful in some models for cutting slits or small windows. This should be done before the children's craft session. Just make the appropriate slits/cuts in all the A4 sheets before pieces are cut out. Rest on a piece of hardboard.

Foldlines – are marked as follows and will be easier to fold if they are very lightly scored before folding.

– – – – – fold outwards (or 'mountain fold')

– · – · – · fold inwards (or 'valley fold')

Tinsel and Glitter – use your initiative to decorate the crib, cards, mobile, decorations, etc, with tinsel or glitter – it really does add a bit of excitement for the children! Glitter glue is less messy than loose glitter.

Contents

1	Crib scene – Mary, Joseph and shepherd	45	Advent calendar – part two
2	Crib scene – three wise men	46	Flight into Egypt – action model
3	Crib scene – baby Jesus, manger, gold and frankincense	47	Fold-out crib scene – Joseph
		48	Fold-out crib scene – Mary and baby Jesus
4	Crib scene – animals and star	49	Fold-out crib scene – stable
5	Crib scene – stable base	50	Fold-out crib scene – shepherds
6	Crib scene – stable roof	51	Fold-out crib scene – angels
7	Crib scene – stable left side	52	Fold-out crib scene – fields
8	Crib scene – stable right side	53	Fold-out crib scene – wise man 1
9	Crib scene – stable pillars	54	Fold-out crib scene – wise men 2 and 3
10	Stand-up nativity card	55	Fold-out crib scene – Bethlehem
11	Angels and shepherds card pop-out	56	3-D star Advent calendar mobile – part one
12	Stand-up angel Christmas card	57	3-D star Advent calendar mobile – part two
13	Christmas tree model	58	3-D star Advent calendar mobile – part three
14	Light of the world Christmas lantern	59	3-D star Advent calendar mobile – part four
15	Christmas angel model	60	Advent action – Jesus is coming: 1. Promised so long
16	Christmas crown – names of Jesus		
17	Christmas plate decoration	61	Advent action – Jesus is coming: 2. Needed so much
18	Walking shepherd		
19	Angels and shepherds – action model	62	Advent action – Jesus is coming: 3. So many signs
20	Christmas frieze – Gabriel tells Mary about Jesus' birth		
		63	Advent action – Jesus is coming: 4. Back so soon
21	Christmas frieze – Mary and Joseph go to Bethlehem		
		64	Gabriel tells Mary about Jesus' birth – action model
22	Christmas frieze – Jesus is born in the stable		
23	Christmas frieze – angels appear to the shepherds	65	Christmas alphabet frieze – part one
		66	Christmas alphabet frieze – part two
24	Christmas frieze – wise men follow the star	67	Christmas alphabet frieze – part three
25	Christmas frieze – storylines for pictures 20-24	68	Christmas alphabet frieze – part four
26	Prophecies about Jesus' birth – spinner part one	69	Christmas alphabet frieze – part five
		70	Christmas alphabet frieze – part six
27	Prophecies about Jesus' birth – spinner part two	71	Christmas alphabet frieze – part seven
		72	Bethlehem fold-up Christmas card
28	An angel tells Zechariah about the birth of John – action model	73	Candle Christmas card
		74	Pop-up star Christmas card
29	No room at the inn – action model	75	Christmas story spinner – part one
30	Angels and dreams in the Christmas story – spinner	76	Christmas story spinner – part two
		77	Christmas gift box
31	Pop-up stable Christmas card – figures and roof	78	Christmas mini gift bag
		79	Christmas fan decoration
32	Pop-up stable Christmas card – base	80	Christmas crown mobile
33	Wise men follow the star – action model	81	Wise men present gifts – action model
34	Simeon and Anna – action model	82	Wise men tube models – part one
35	A. Expanding angel decoration B. Dove of Peace tree decoration	83	Wise men tube models – part two
		84	Camel mask
36	A. Expanding angel – body B. Dove of Peace – wings	85	God speaks to Joseph in dreams – action model
37	Christmas mobile – stable roof	86	Christmas stained glass window – part one
38	Christmas mobile – star, baby Jesus, animals	87	Christmas stained glass window – part two
39	Christmas mobile – Mary, Joseph, king, shepherd	88	Pop-up kings Christmas card – part one
		89	Pop-up kings Christmas card – part two
40	Sheep face baseball cap	90	Christmas story map puzzle
41	Christmas window picture	91	Christmas quiz-search
42	Christmas crossword	92	Christmas story – find the order puzzle
43	Christmas puzzle page		
44	Advent calendar – part one		

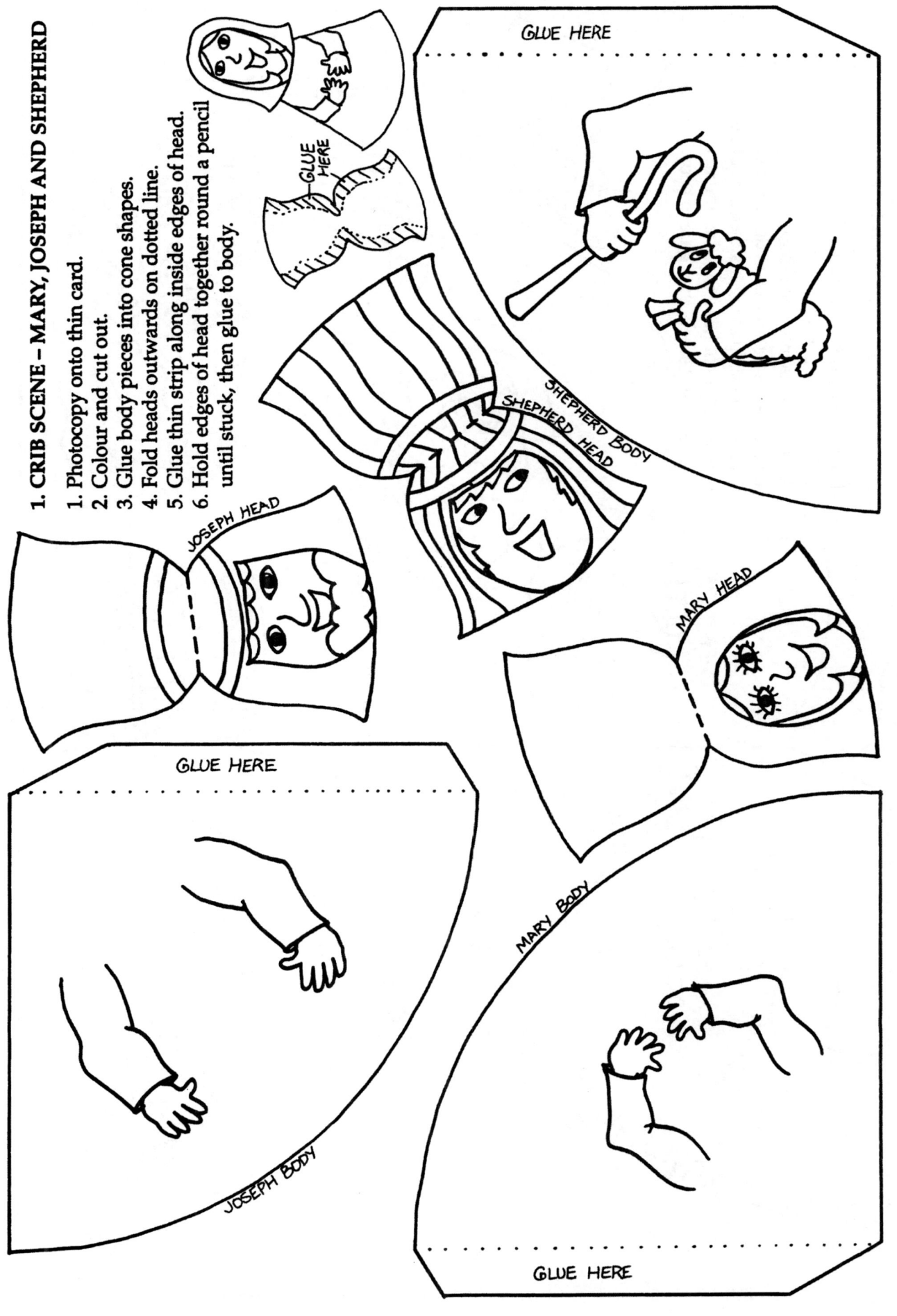

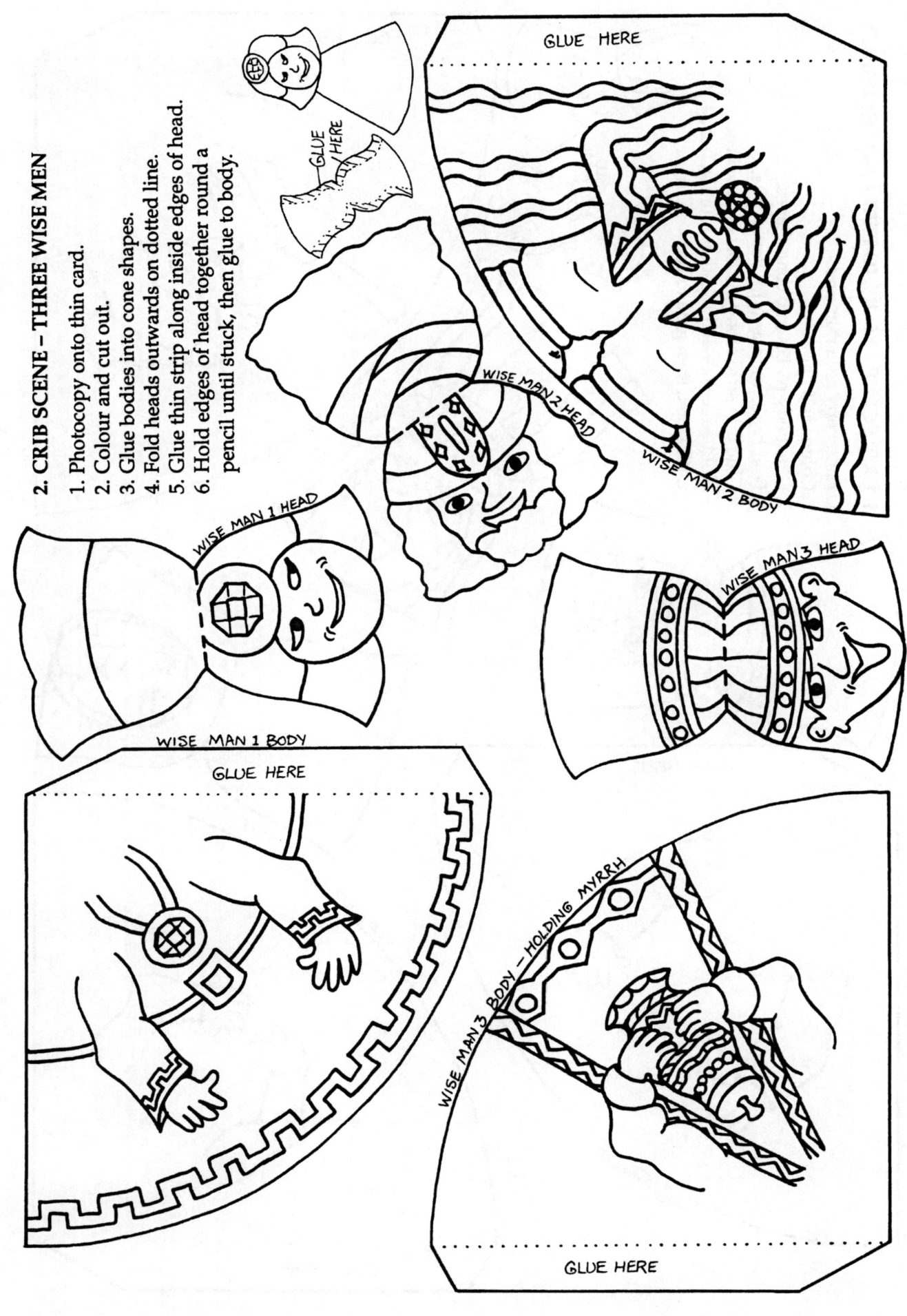

2. CRIB SCENE – THREE WISE MEN

1. Photocopy onto thin card.
2. Colour and cut out.
3. Glue bodies into cone shapes.
4. Fold heads outwards on dotted line.
5. Glue thin strip along inside edges of head.
6. Hold edges of head together round a pencil until stuck, then glue to body.

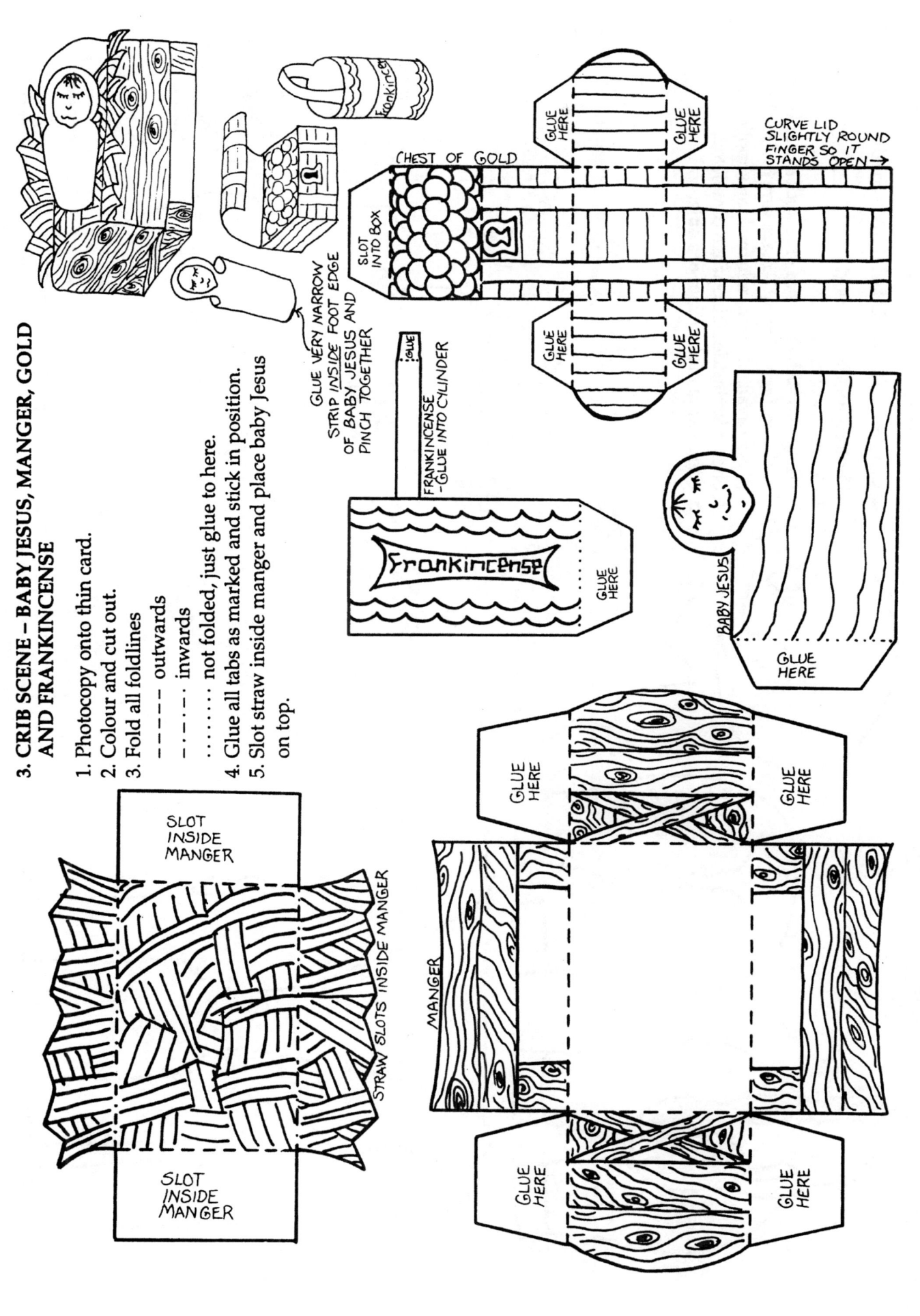

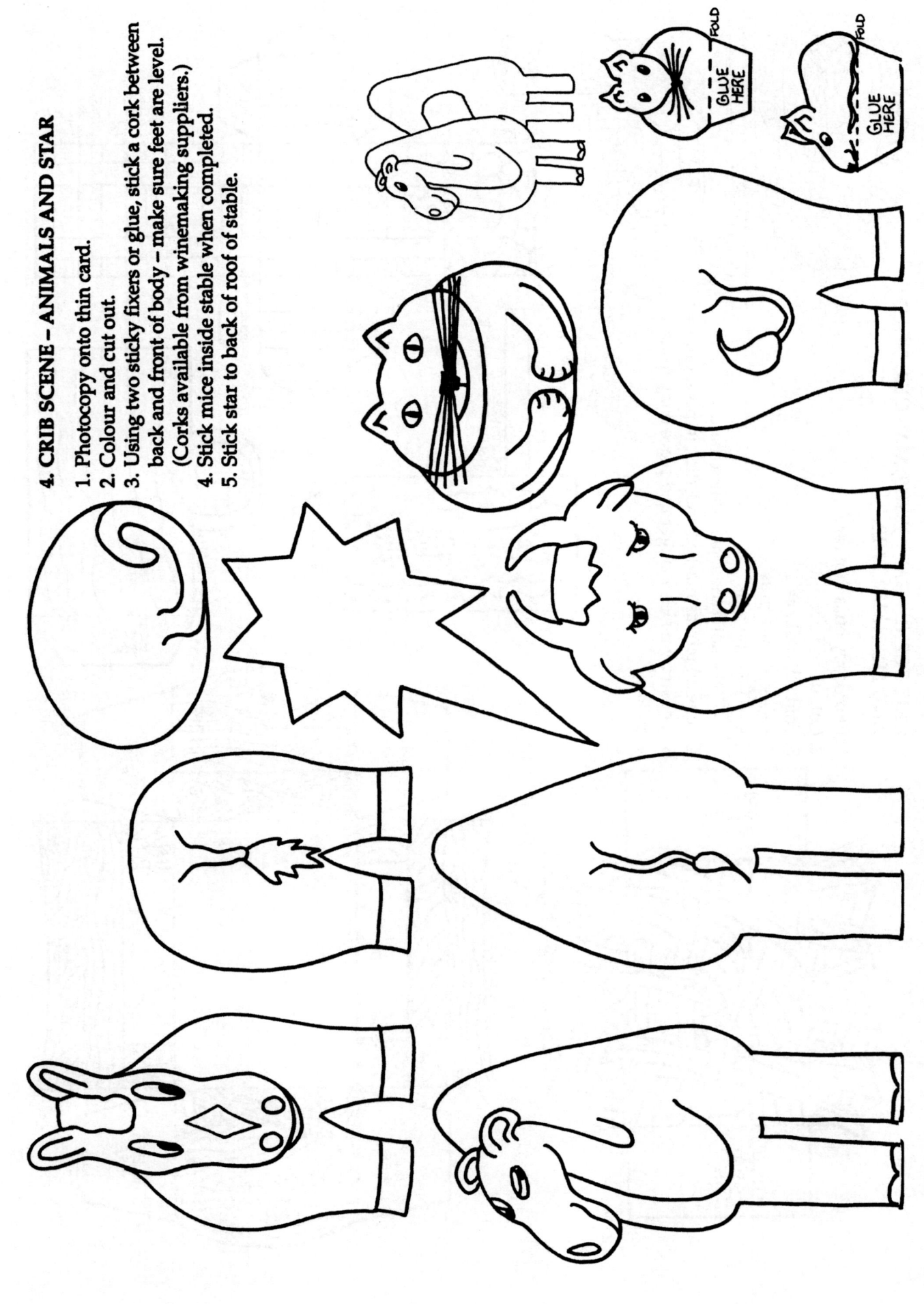

5. CRIB SCENE – STABLE BASE
1. Photocopy onto card and cut out. 2. Cut all slots as marked (by adult using craft knife).

P — GLUE STABLE ROOF TAB HERE — Q

H ⌐
I ⌐
W ⌐
X ⌐
J ⌐
K ⌐

L ⌐
M ⌐
Y ⌐
Z ⌐
N ⌐
O ⌐

FOLD IN

A ⌐
B ⌐

C ⌐
D ⌐

GLUE PILLAR HERE

GLUE PILLAR HERE

6. **CRIB SCENE – STABLE ROOF** 1. Photocopy onto thin card. 2. Colour and cut out. 3. Fold out on all dotted − − − − foldlines. 4. Glue two small tabs under front edges of roof eaves. 5. Glue long back tab PQ to top back of stable wall.

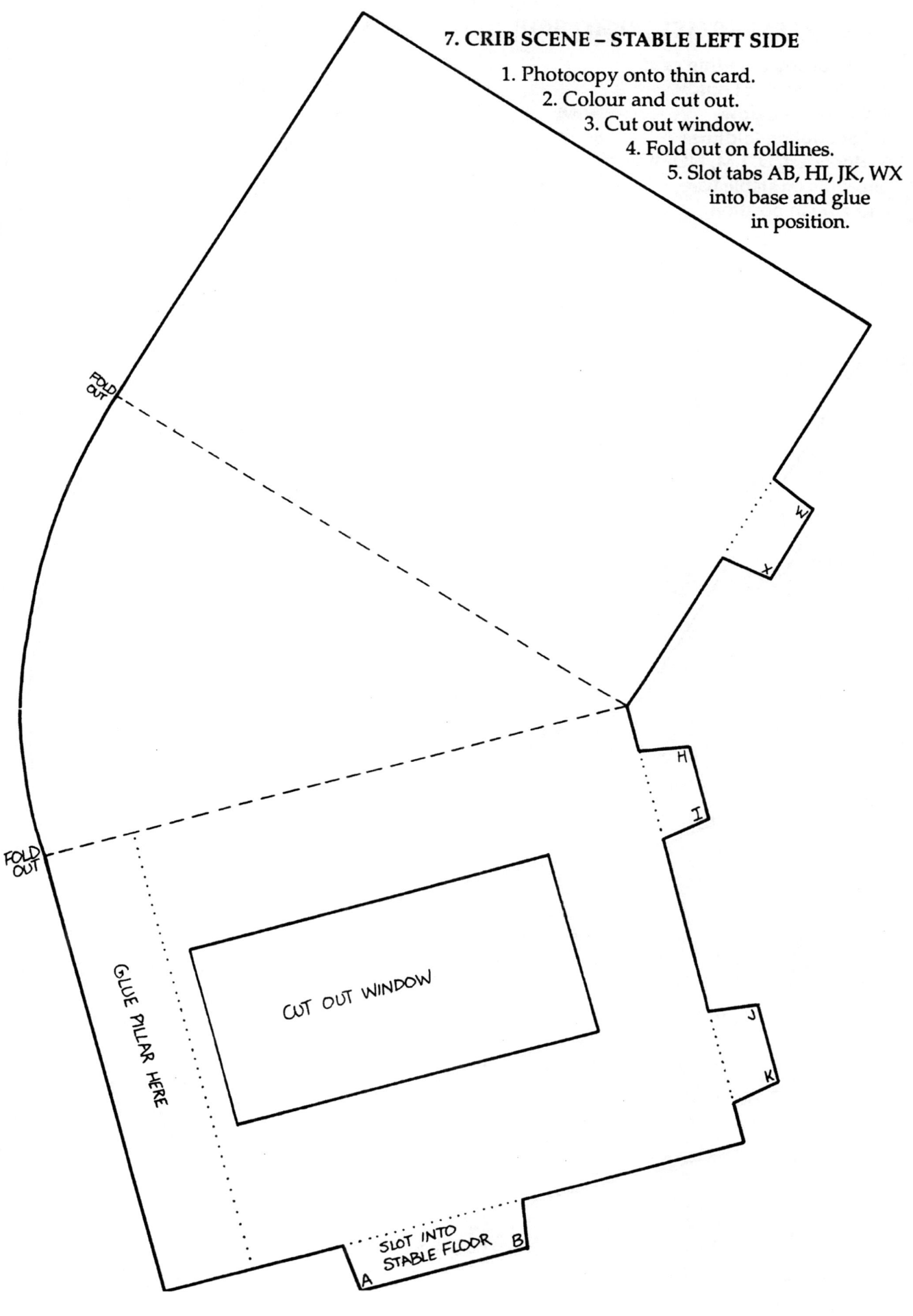

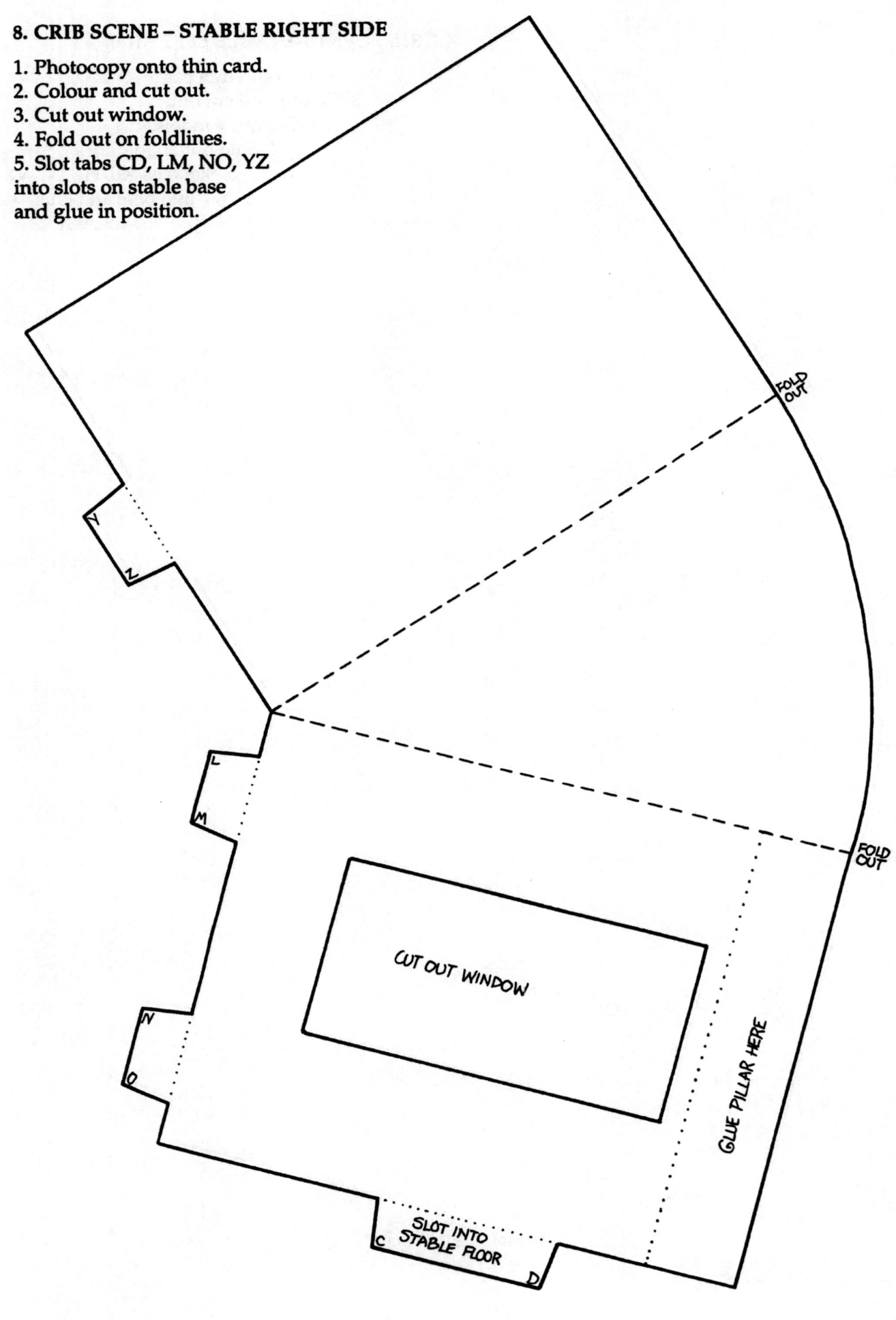

9. CRIB SCENE – STABLE PILLARS

1. Photocopy onto thin card.
2. Colour and cut out.
3. Fold out on all foldlines - - - - -
4. Glue one long side and base of each pillar and glue in position on stable base and against side wall.

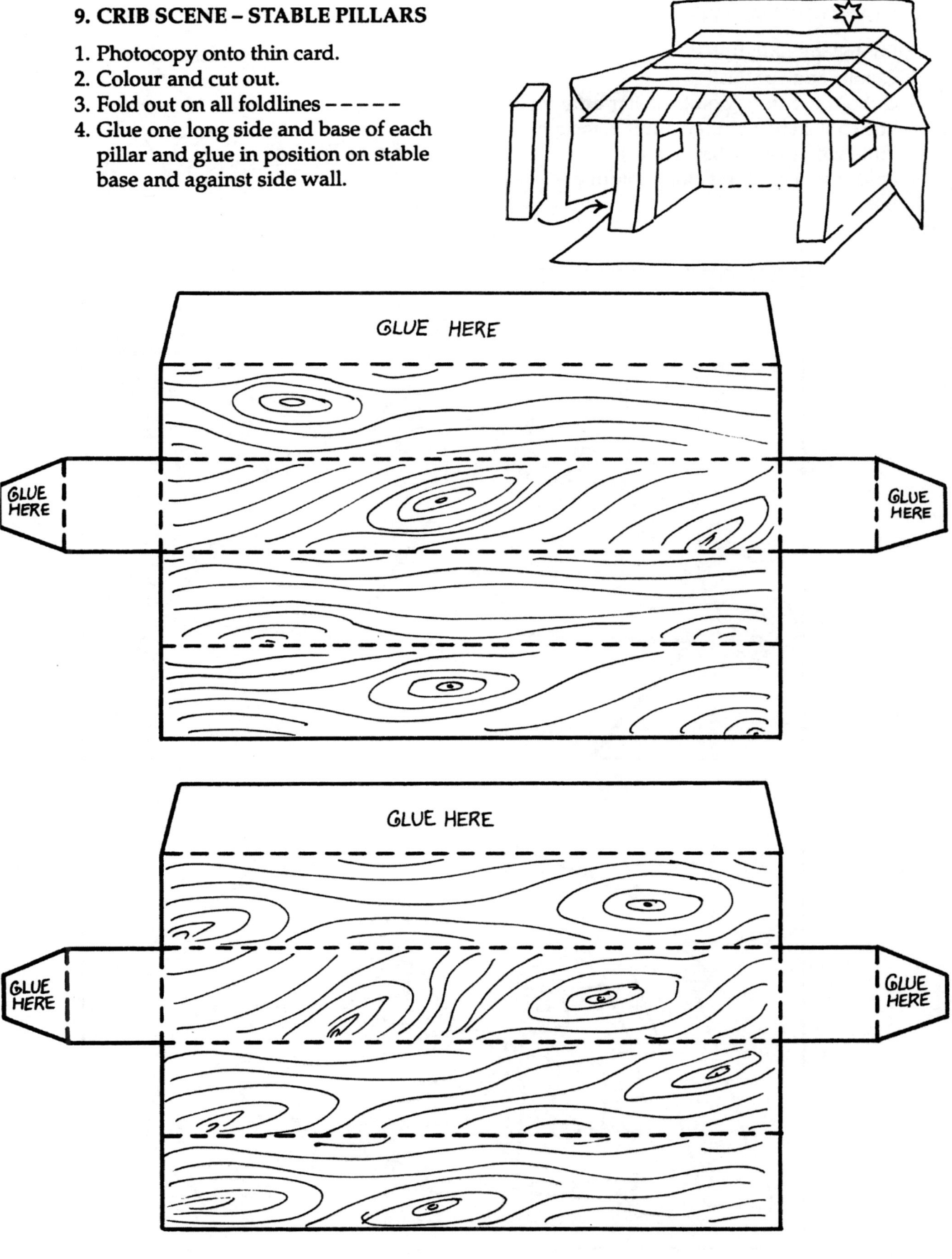

10. STAND-UP NATIVITY CARD

1. Photocopy onto thin card.
2. Colour and cut out.
3. Cut out top three points of star **only** on thick line so it stands out (an adult using a craft knife will give the best result).
4. Fold rest of card out along foldline - - - - -

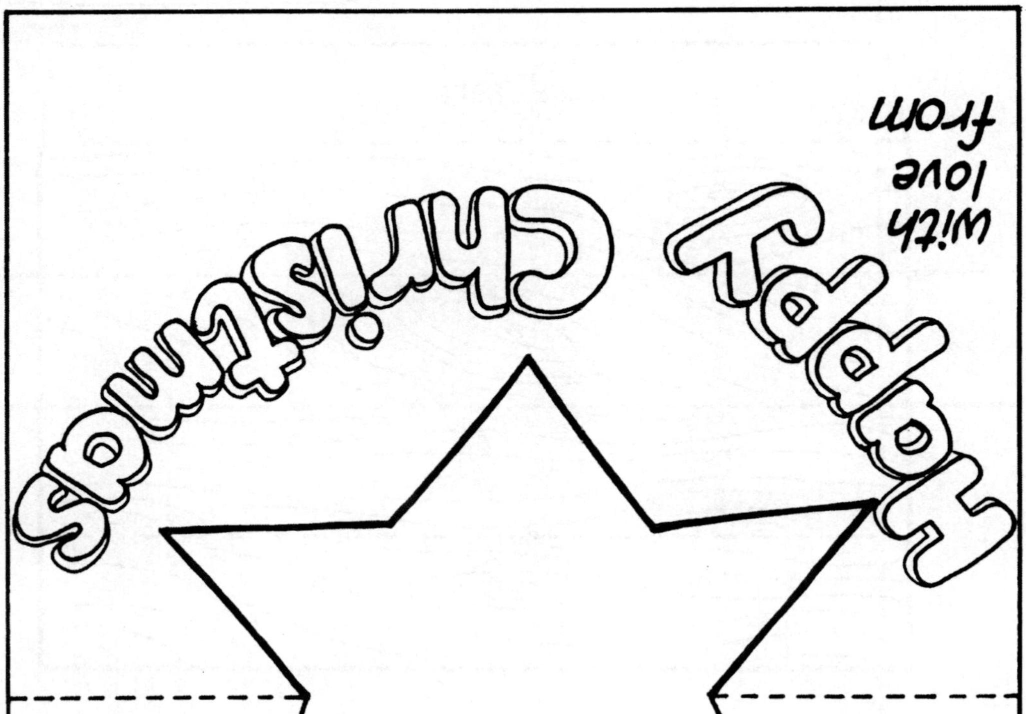

12. STAND-UP ANGEL CHRISTMAS CARD

1. Photocopy onto thin card.
2. Colour and cut out.
3. Cut round shoulders and head of angel on thick black line so it will stand out. (Best done by an adult using a craft knife.)
4. Fold rest of card along foldline.

Happy Christmas

with love from

A Saviour has been born to you; he is Christ the Lord

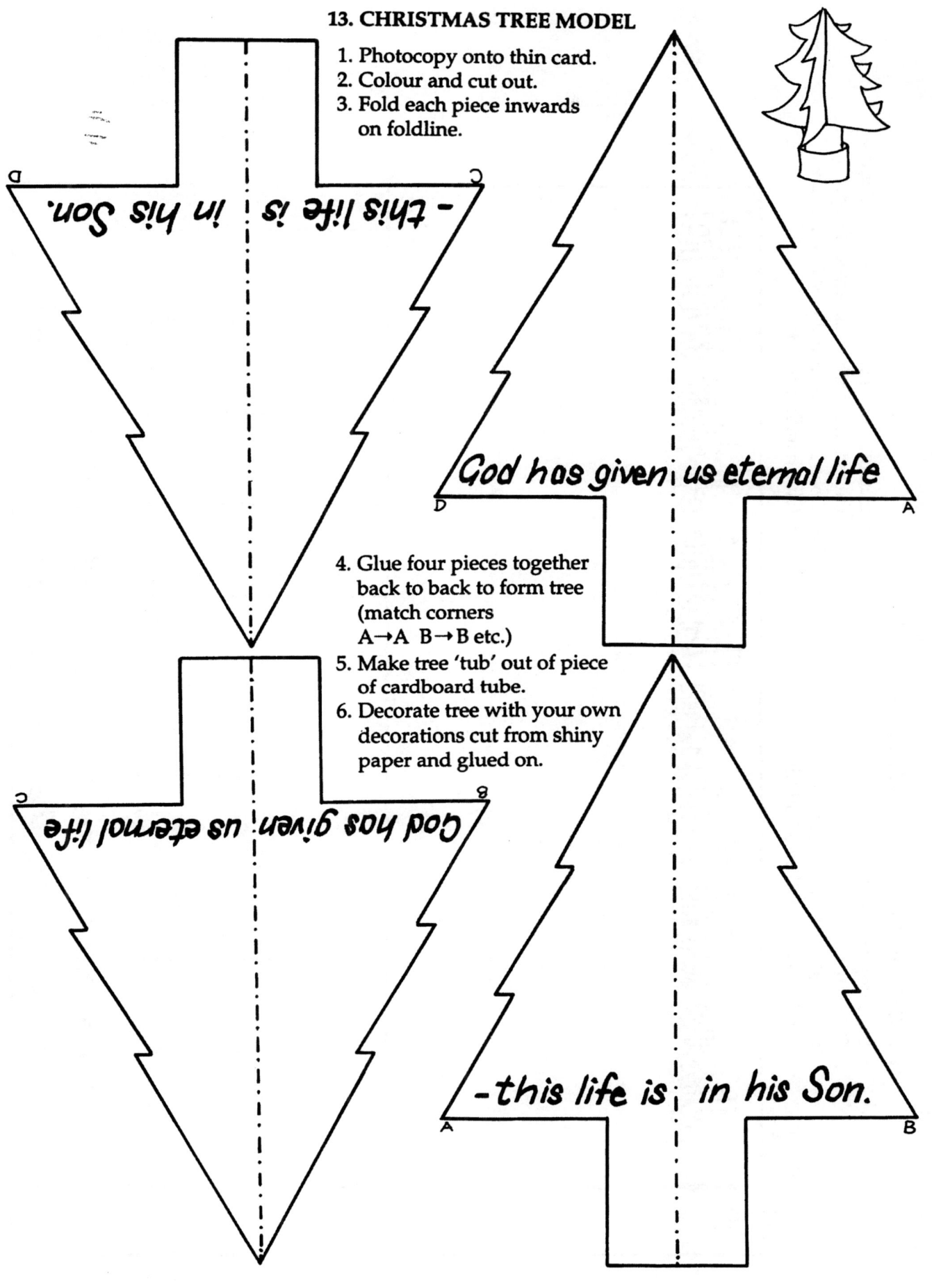

13. CHRISTMAS TREE MODEL

1. Photocopy onto thin card.
2. Colour and cut out.
3. Fold each piece inwards on foldline.
4. Glue four pieces together back to back to form tree (match corners A→A B→B etc.)
5. Make tree 'tub' out of piece of cardboard tube.
6. Decorate tree with your own decorations cut from shiny paper and glued on.

14. LIGHT OF THE WORLD CHRISTMAS LANTERN

1. Photocopy onto paper.
2. Decorate lantern and cut out.
3. Cut off strip at end for handle.
4. Fold lantern in half along foldline -----.
5. Cut all parallel slits marked by solid line – cut through both thicknesses of paper.
6. Open lantern out and glue into cylinder.
7. Glue handle onto top.

Jesus said: I am the Light of the World

Whoever follows me will never walk in darkness, but will have the light of life. *John 3 v 12*

CUT OFF HERE
HANDLE GLUE
GLUE HERE
FOLD OUT
GLUE HERE
GLUE

15. CHRISTMAS ANGEL MODEL

1. Photocopy onto paper.
2. Cut out circle.
3. Draw pattern on wings front and back. Colour in angel.
4. Cut down centre back thick black line and around head but taking care **not** to cut through neck.
5. Fold in on foldlines –··–··– and staple dotted foldlines together so angel body forms a cone shape.

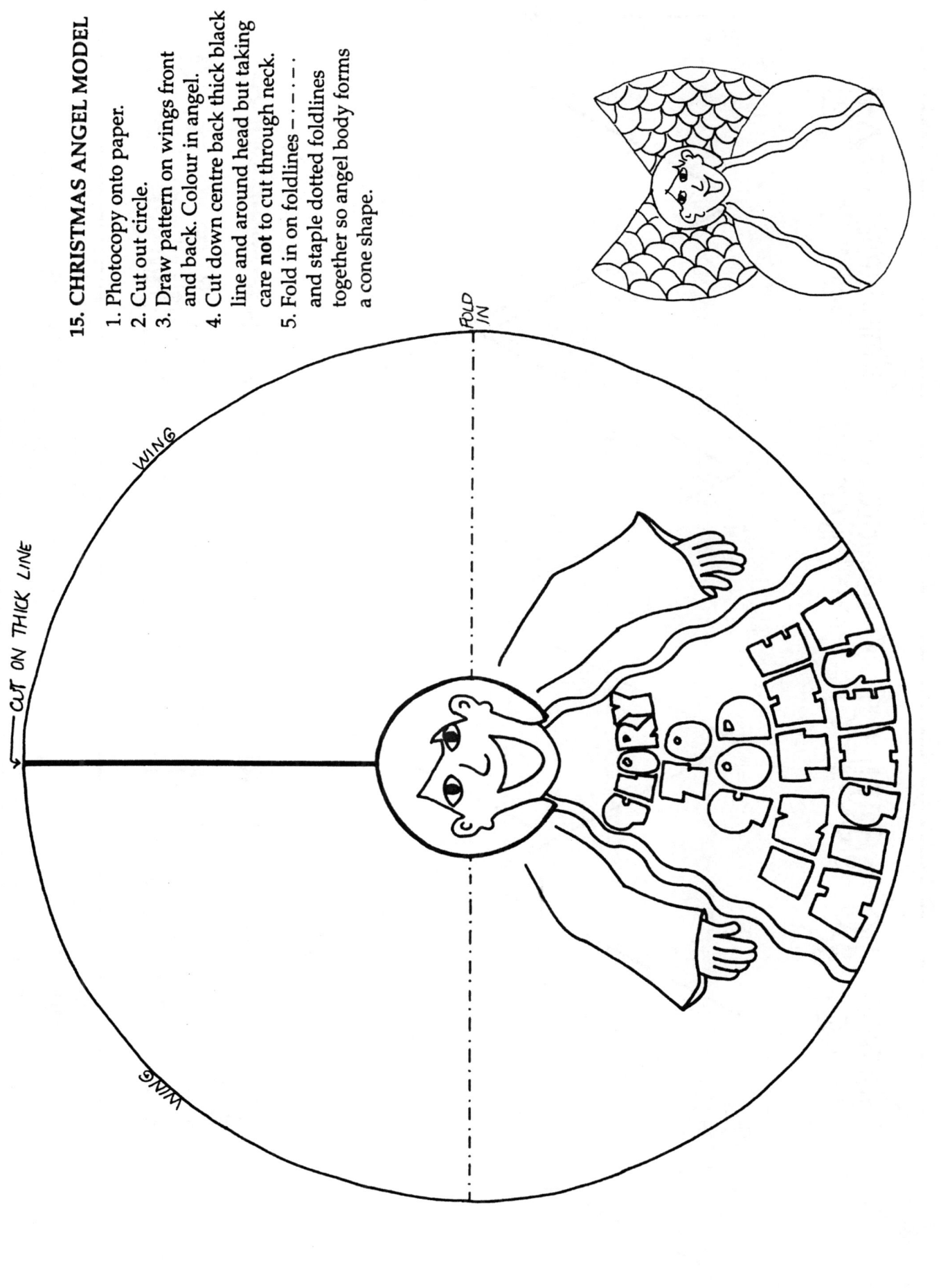

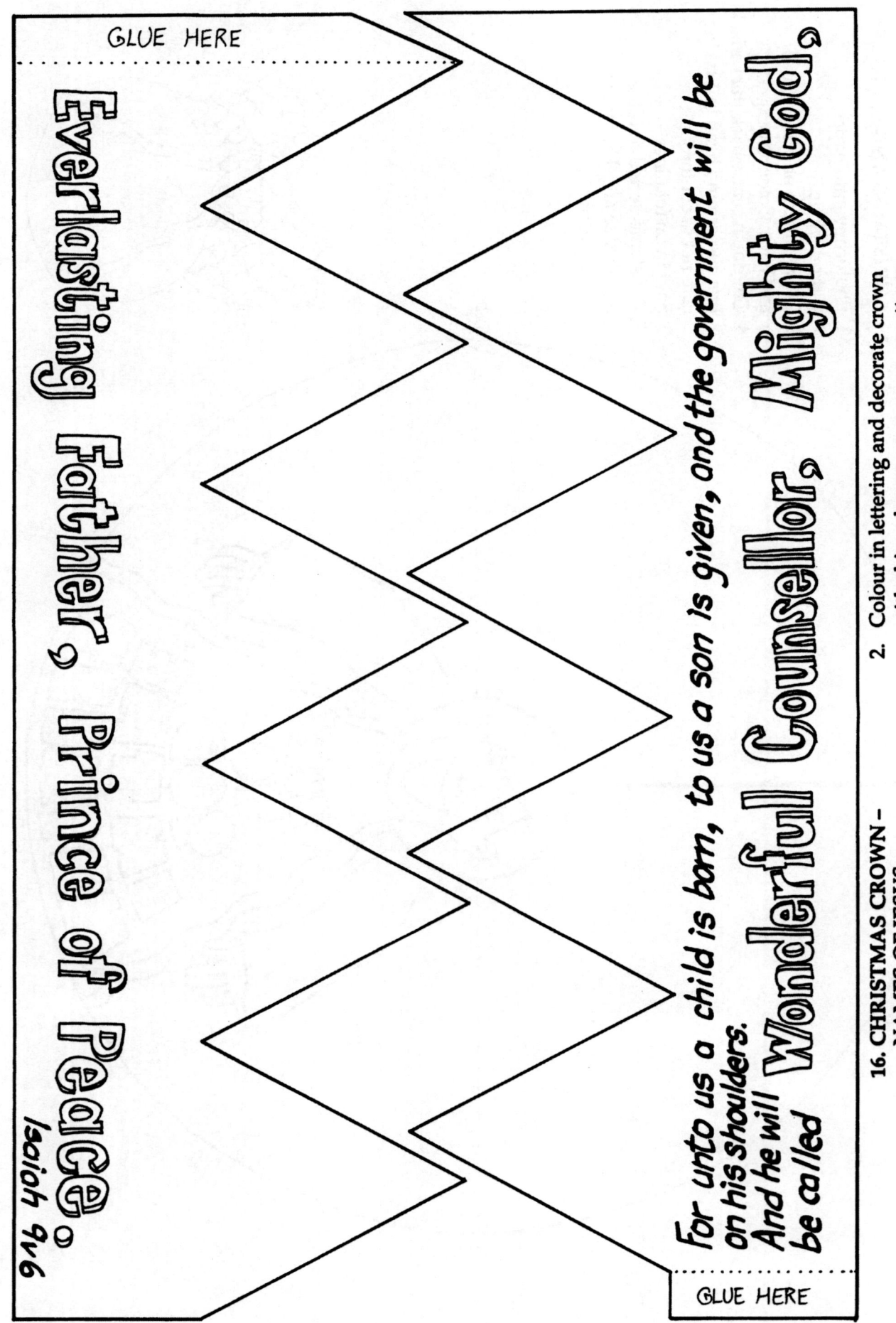

16. CHRISTMAS CROWN – NAMES OF JESUS

1. Photocopy onto thin card.
2. Colour in lettering and decorate crown with shiny shapes or your own pattern.
3. Cut out and glue together.

17. CHRISTMAS PLATE DECORATION

1. Photocopy onto thin card.
2. Colour and cut out.
3. Decorate the rim of a large paper plate with your own pattern.
4. Stick the pieces onto the plate using sticky fixers (better than glue, as they give a slight stand-out effect).
5. Staple some tinsel to the top of the plate.

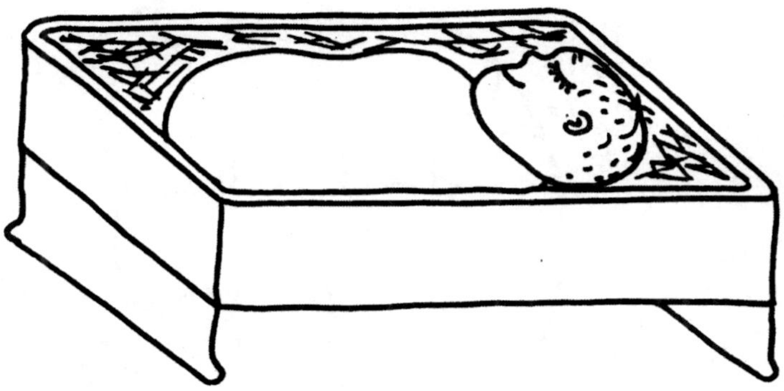

18. WALKING SHEPHERD

1. Photocopy onto thin card.
2. Colour and cut out.
3. Glue 'foot' circles together back to back.
4. Pierce dots A, B, C, D – put paper fastener through A, B, C, D.
5. Staple top of head together.

Let's go to Bethlehem and see this thing that has happened, which the Lord has told us about.

19. ANGELS AND SHEPHERDS – ACTION MODEL

1. Photocopy onto thin card.
2. Colour in and cut out all pieces – cut off long strip along RS line.
3. Cut slits AB and CD.
4. With long strip, slot PR into AB and QS into CD.
5. Glue clouds in position as marked – glue under end tab of cloud beyond foldline only.
   Cloud X lies **under** cloud Y at overlap of edges.
6. Start with shepherds at slit CD.
7. Open cloud Y then X so angels appear, then pull PR so shepherds go to Bethlehem!

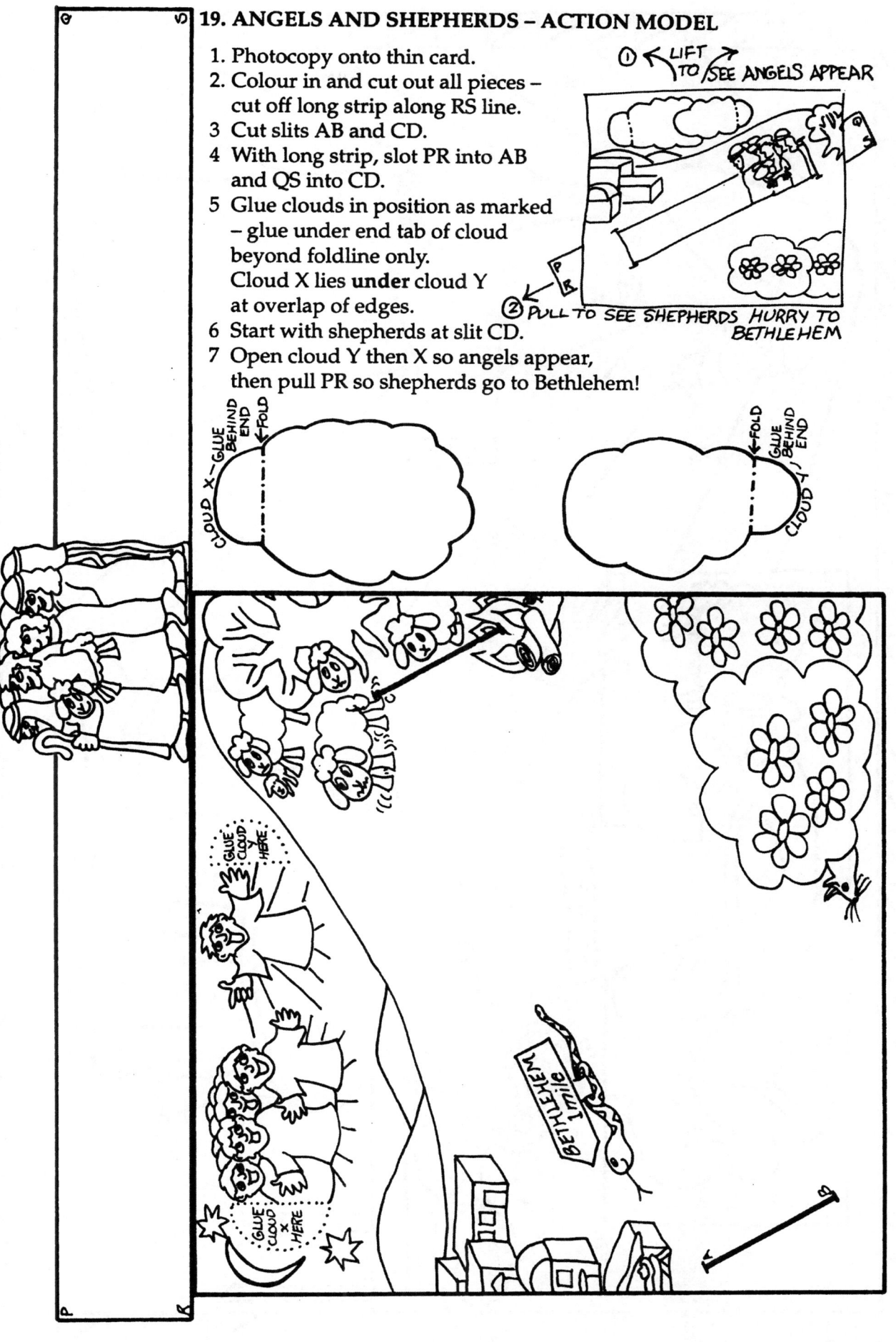

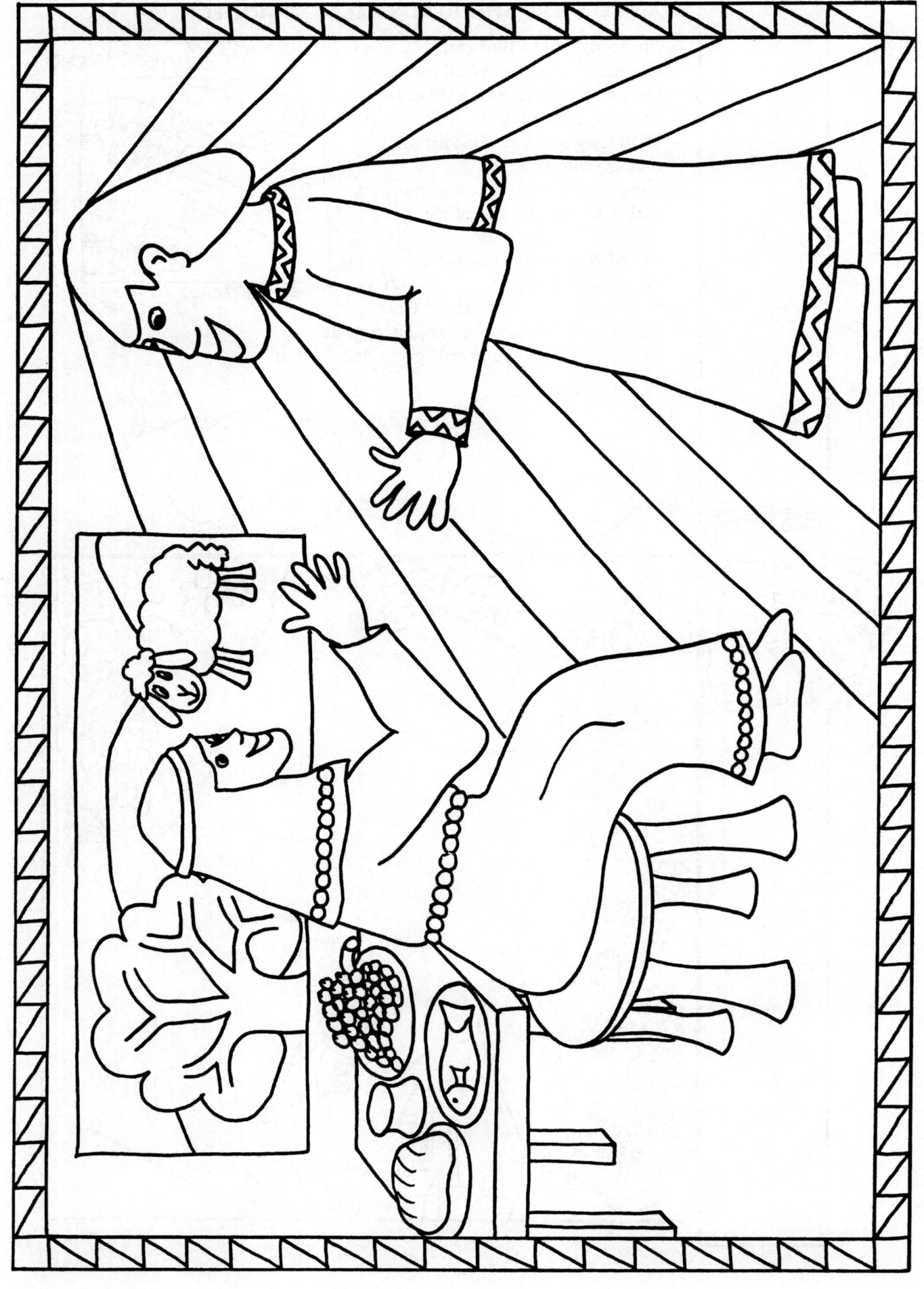

21.

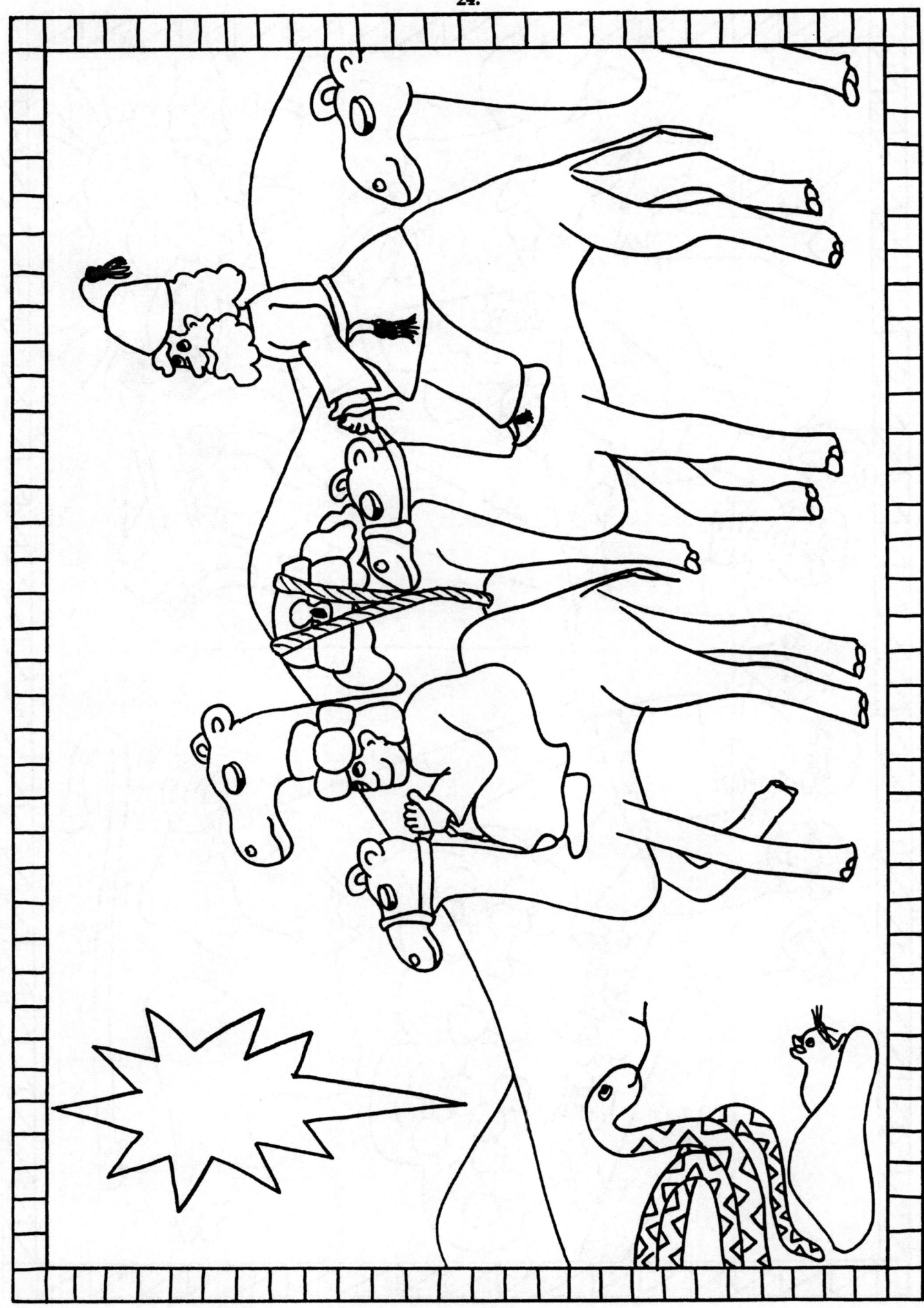

25.

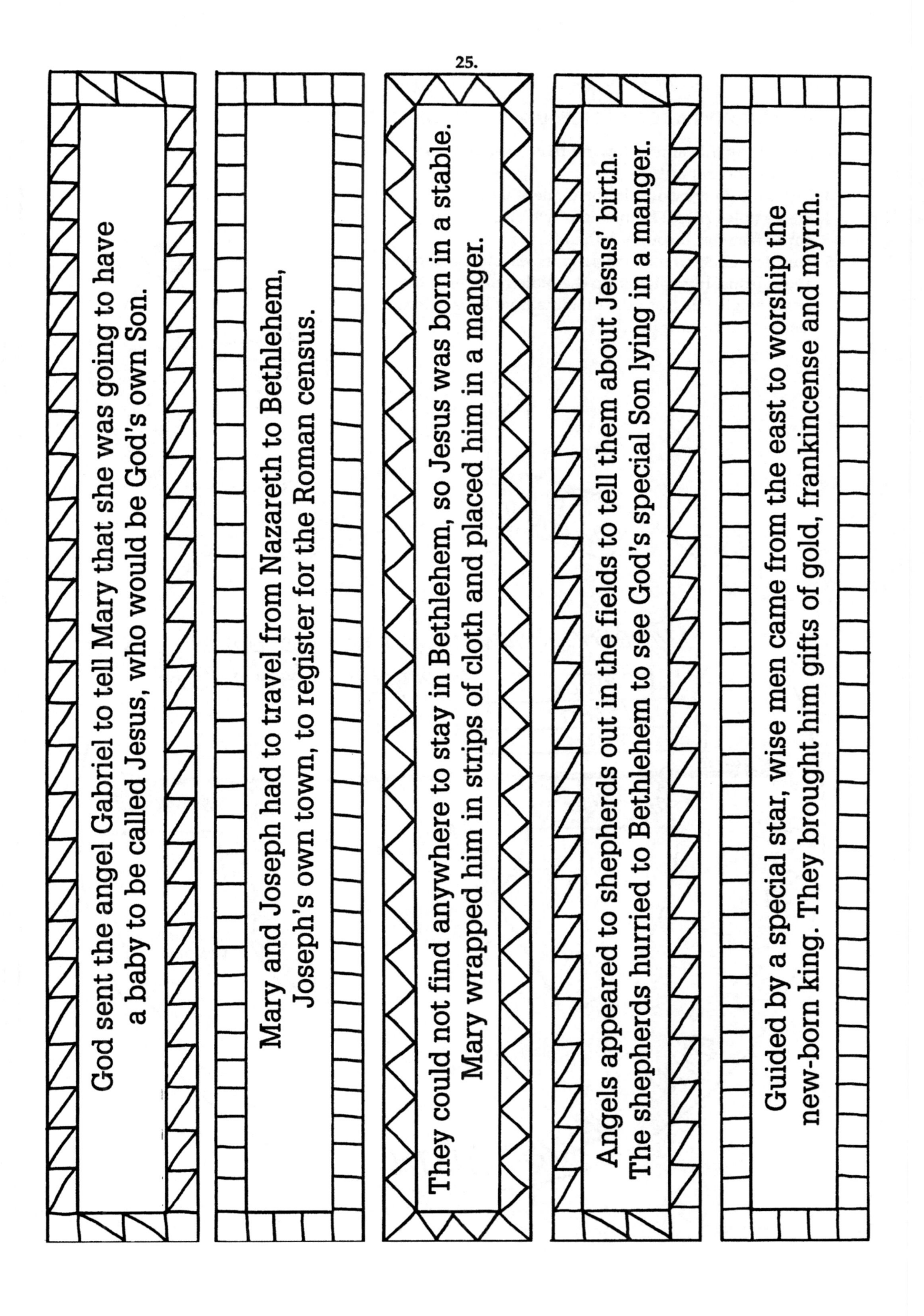

God sent the angel Gabriel to tell Mary that she was going to have a baby to be called Jesus, who would be God's own Son.

Mary and Joseph had to travel from Nazareth to Bethlehem, Joseph's own town, to register for the Roman census.

They could not find anywhere to stay in Bethlehem, so Jesus was born in a stable. Mary wrapped him in strips of cloth and placed him in a manger.

Angels appeared to shepherds out in the fields to tell them about Jesus' birth. The shepherds hurried to Bethlehem to see God's special Son lying in a manger.

Guided by a special star, wise men came from the east to worship the new-born king. They brought him gifts of gold, frankincense and myrrh.

26. PROPHECIES ABOUT JESUS' BIRTH – SPINNER PART ONE

1. Photocopy this and following page onto thin card.
2. Colour and cut out.
3. Cut out two windows in top circle (this page).
4. Pierce holes A and B, then join two circles with paper fastener through A then B.
5. Turn top circle to read off prophecies and fulfilments about Jesus' birth. Look up the bible references for more detail. See from the timeline how long before Jesus the prophets lived.

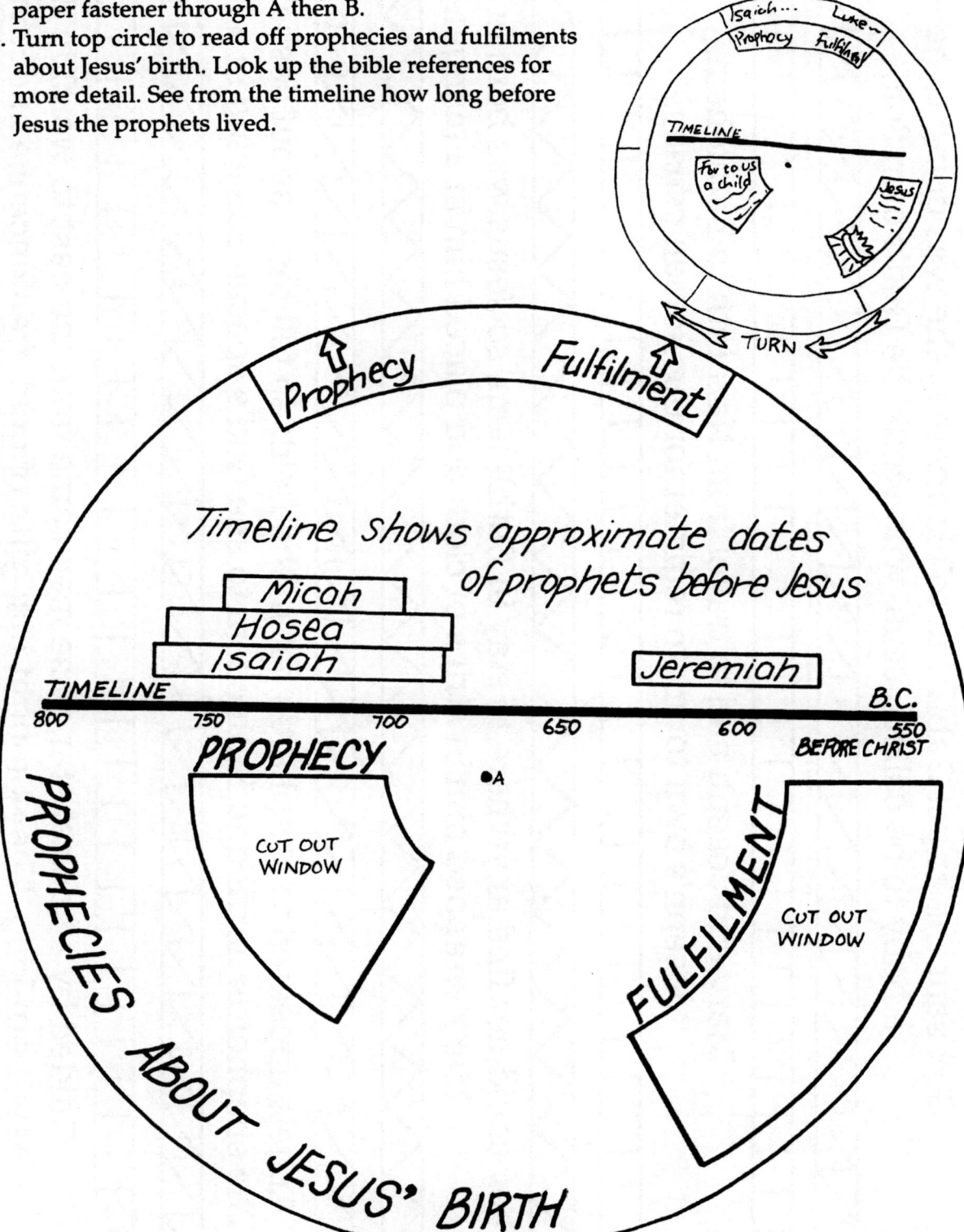

27. PROPHECIES ABOUT JESUS' BIRTH – SPINNER PART TWO

See previous page for instructions.

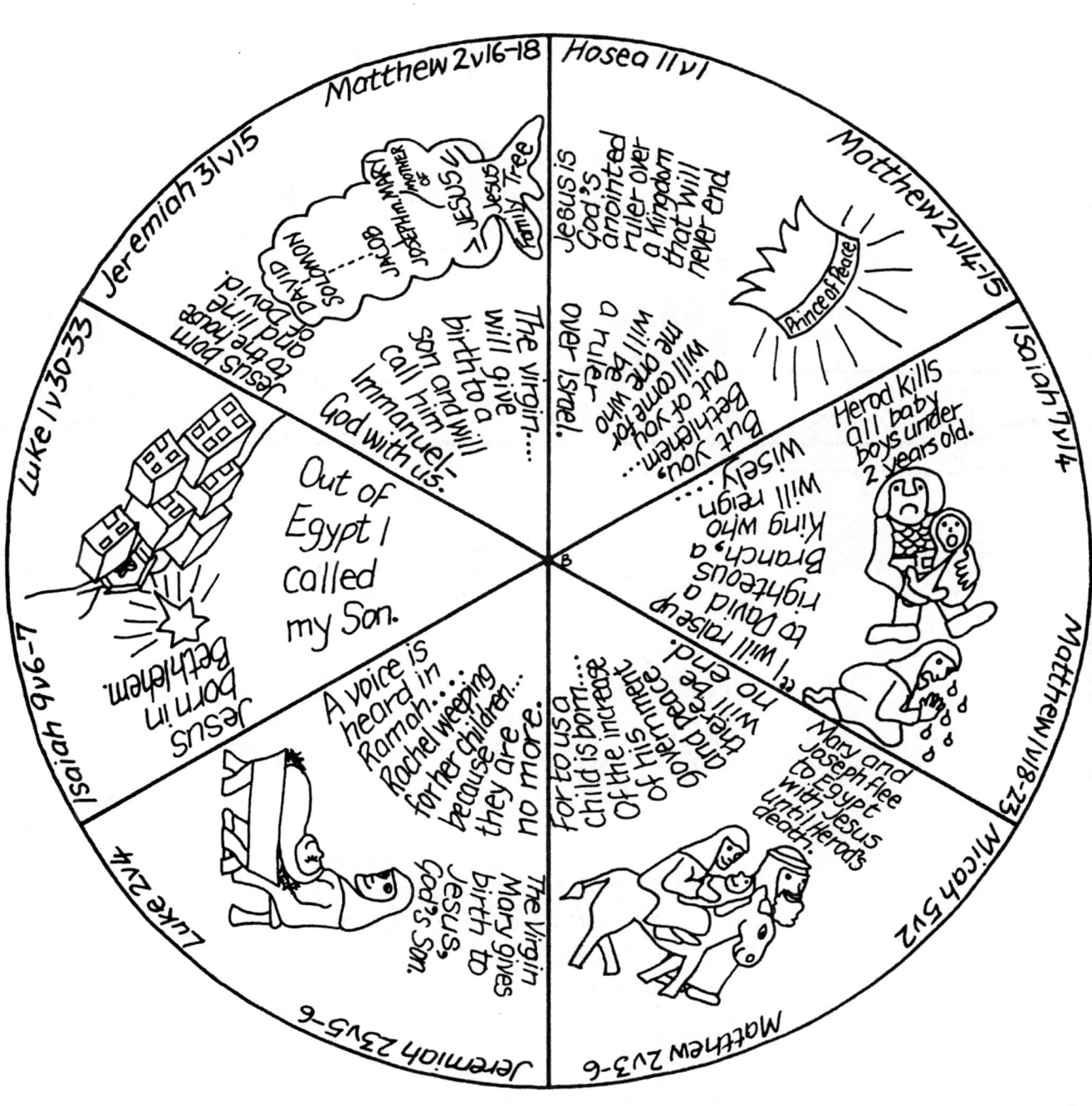

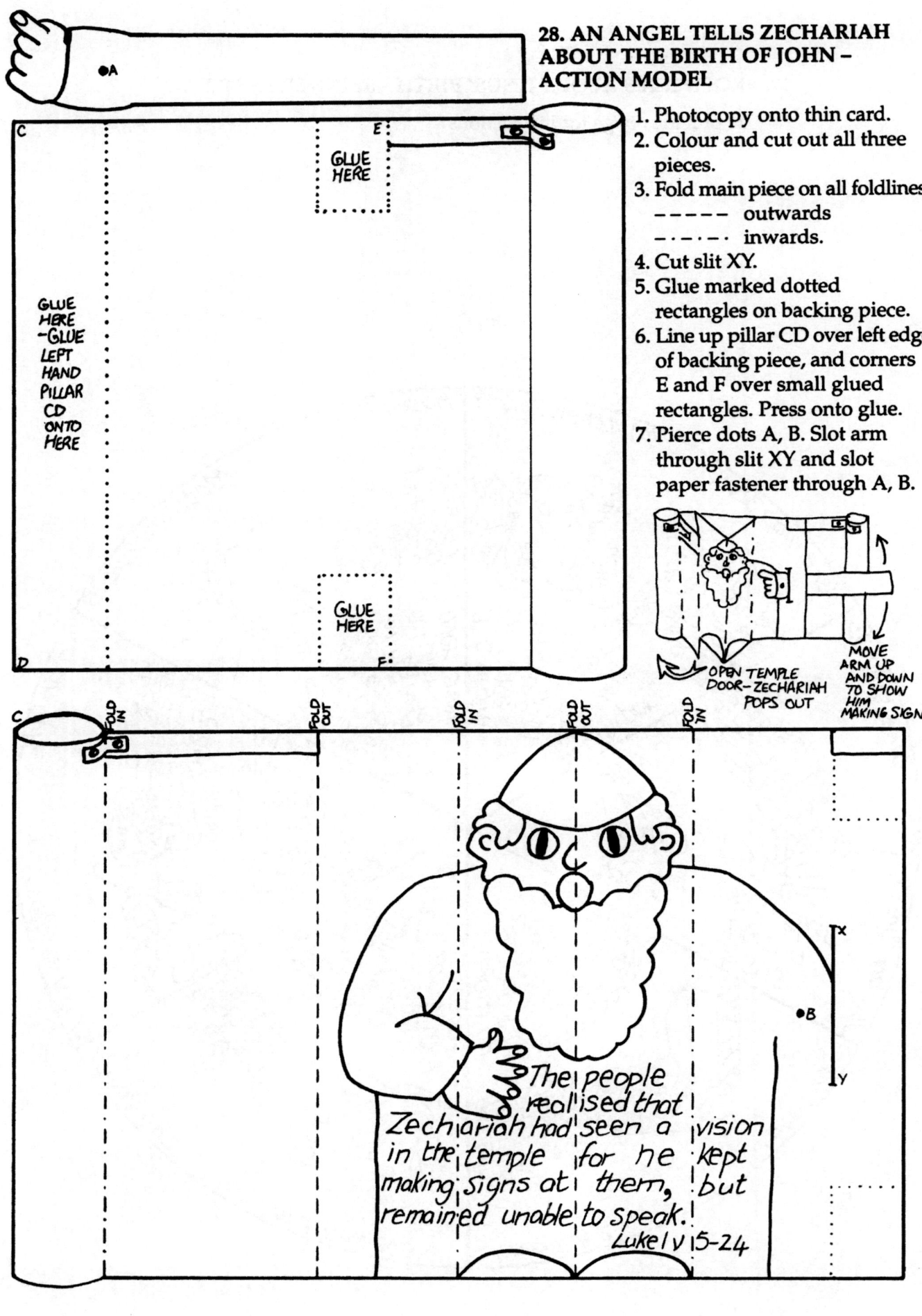

29. NO ROOM AT THE INN – ACTION MODEL

1. Photocopy onto thin card.
2. Colour and cut out.
3. Cut slits AB and CD.
4. Cut thick black slits round three sides of inn door only and fold along dotted line – – – – so that door opens.
5. Fold inwards on dotted line – · – · – on long strip.
6. Slot end XY of long strip up through slit CD, down through AB, and up through open door.
7. Glue behind folded end XY then glue to inside of door edge XY.

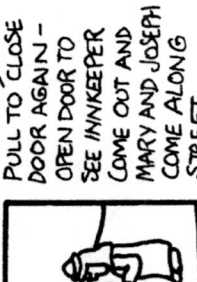

PULL TO CLOSE DOOR AGAIN – OPEN DOOR TO SEE INNKEEPER COME OUT AND MARY AND JOSEPH COME ALONG STREET.

OPEN DOOR

GLUE XY TO INSIDE EDGE

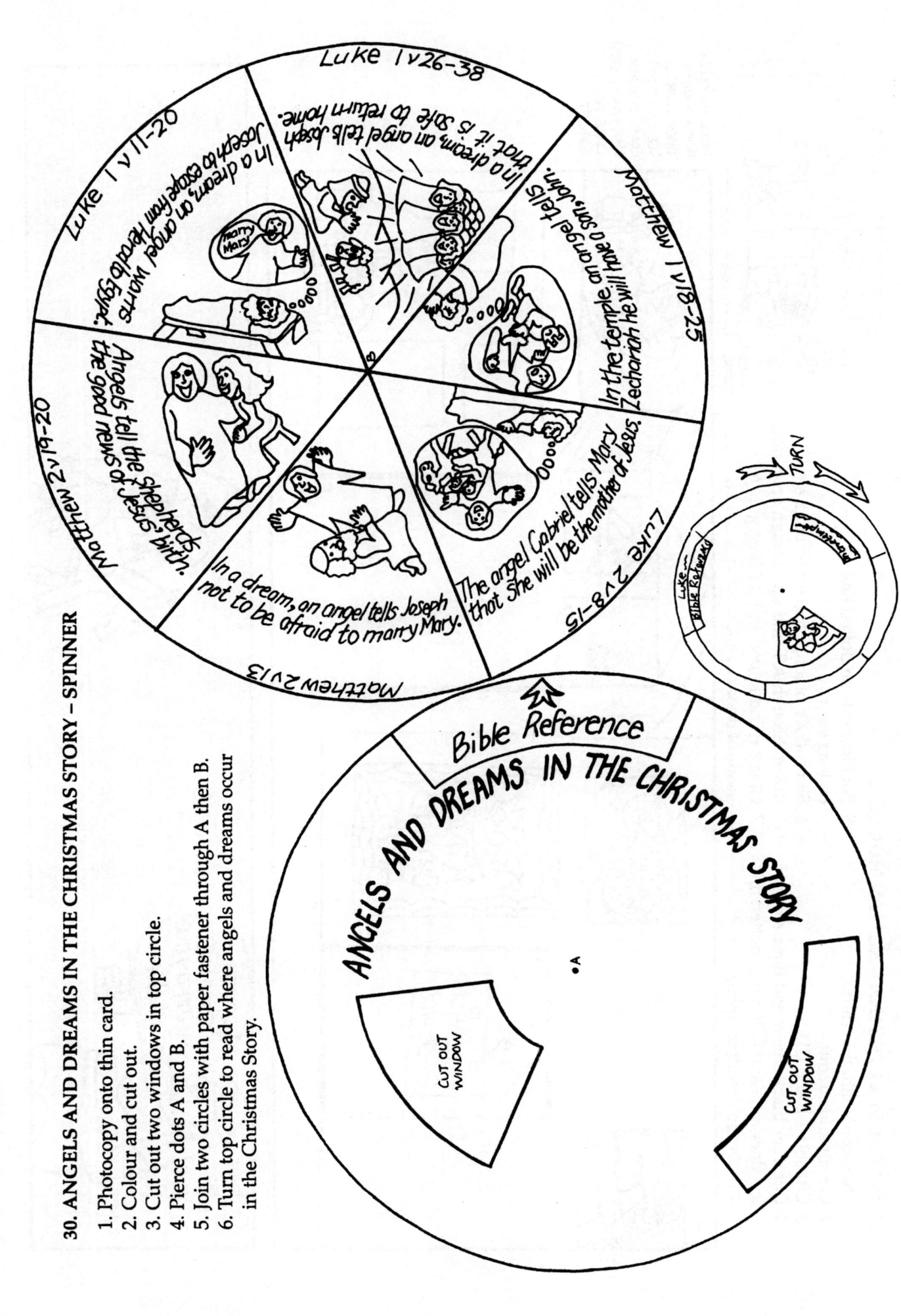

30. ANGELS AND DREAMS IN THE CHRISTMAS STORY – SPINNER

1. Photocopy onto thin card.
2. Colour and cut out.
3. Cut out two windows in top circle.
4. Pierce dots A and B.
5. Join two circles with paper fastener through A then B.
6. Turn top circle to read where angels and dreams occur in the Christmas Story.

31. POP-UP STABLE CHRISTMAS CARD – FIGURES AND ROOF

1. Photocopy this page and following one (32) onto thin card.
2. Cut round outside edge of base.
3. Colour and cut out all pieces on this page.
4. Fold base piece in half first along central line, then open flat again.
5. Cut six slits AB, CD, EF, GH, JK and LM on solid black lines.
6. Carefully fold all dotted lines as shown
    –·–·–· inwards
    – – – – outwards
   so that 3 rectangles stand out from card base as shown.
7. Fold stable roof tab inwards along dotted line and glue to dotted rectangle on base card.
8. Glue Mary and Joseph to box FH.
9. Stick shepherd and star in position using sticky fixers (for 3-D effect).
10. Cut slit XY round donkey face, then glue behind nose and stick looking round RH pillar.

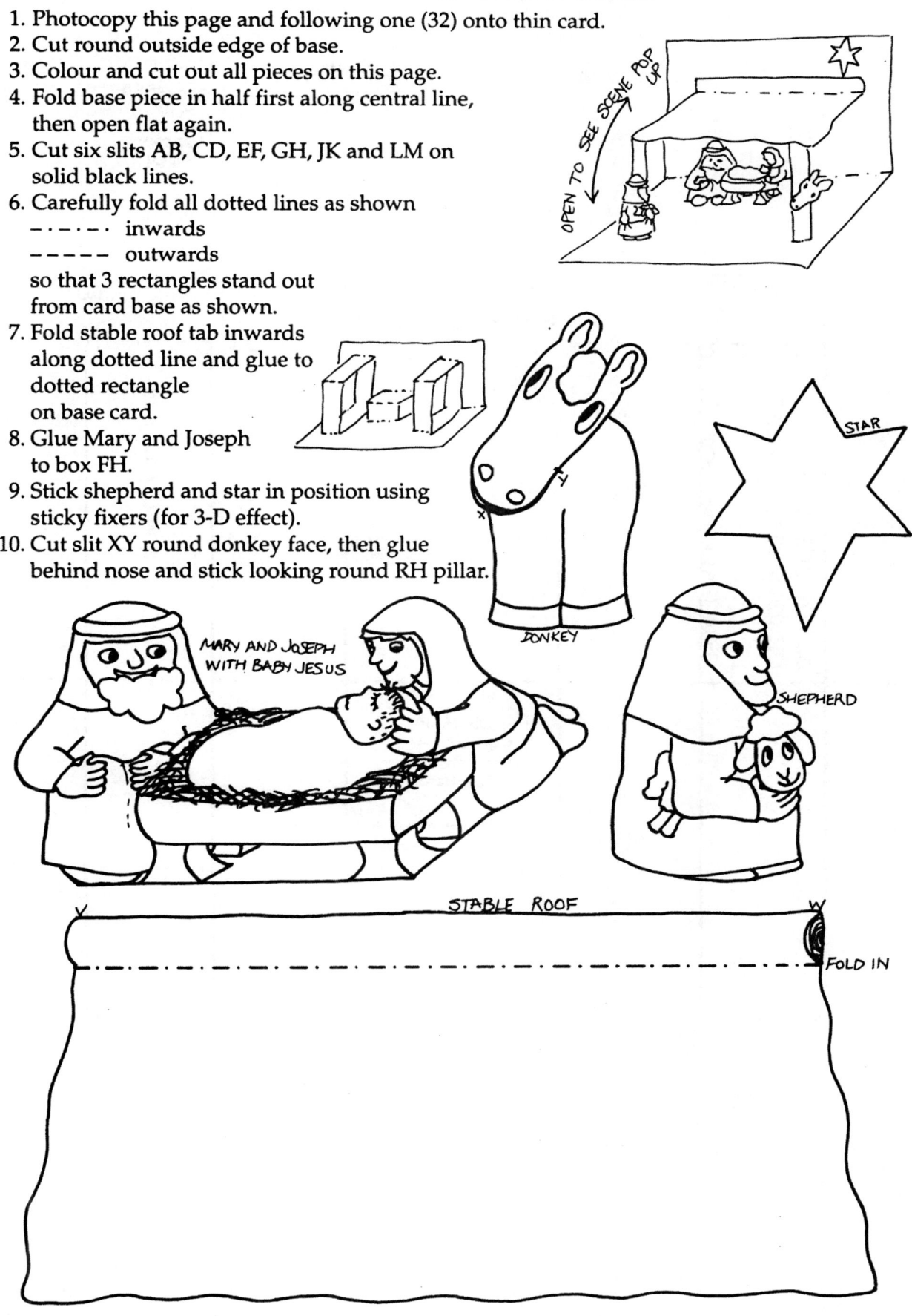

CUT ROUND OUTLINE

STICK STAR
HERE
USING
STICKY
FIXER

V .... W
GLUE STABLE ROOF TAB HERE

A   C   J   L

32. POP-UP STABLE CHRISTMAS CARD – BASE

GLUE STABLE ROOF HERE

GLUE STABLE ROOF HERE

E   G

GLUE MARY
AND JOSEPH
WITH BABY
JESUS HERE.

F .... H

B .... D   K .... M

CUT ROUND OUTLINE

33. WISE MEN FOLLOW THE STAR – ACTION MODEL

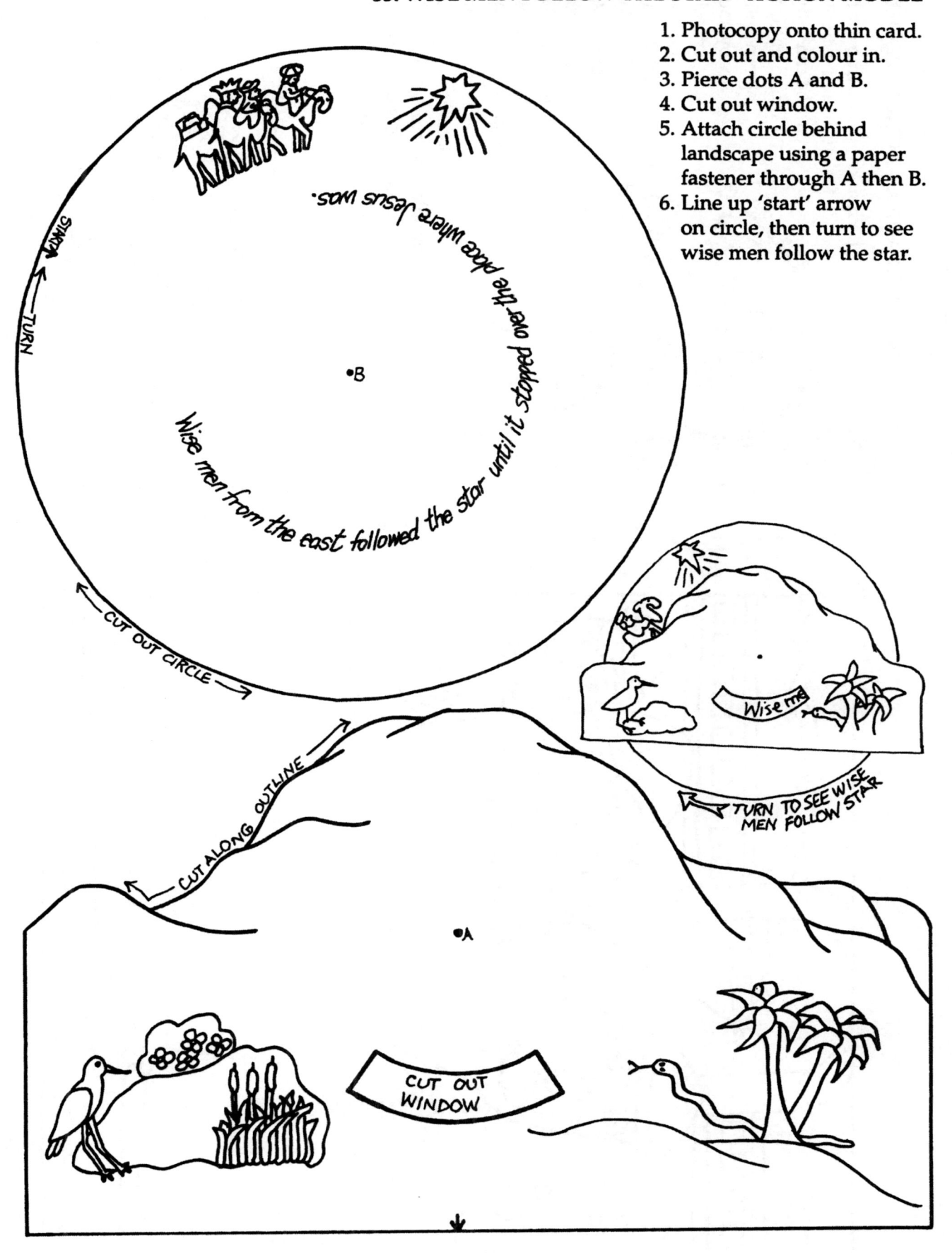

1. Photocopy onto thin card.
2. Cut out and colour in.
3. Pierce dots A and B.
4. Cut out window.
5. Attach circle behind landscape using a paper fastener through A then B.
6. Line up 'start' arrow on circle, then turn to see wise men follow the star.

Wise men from the east followed the star until it stopped over the place where Jesus was.

TURN → START

← CUT OUT CIRCLE

CUT ALONG OUTLINE

CUT OUT WINDOW

TURN TO SEE WISE MEN FOLLOW STAR

Wise me

34. SIMEON AND ANNA – ACTION MODEL

1. Photocopy onto thin card.
2. Colour in and cut out, cutting carefully round outline of arm with baby and speech bubble.
3. Cut slits VW and XYZ.
4. Pierce dots A and B.
5. Slot arm with baby up through slit VW from behind picture and speech bubble top through slit XYZ.
6. Join pieces using paper fastener through A then B.

"Lord, my eyes have seen your salvation."

PUSH TO SEE SIMEON LIFT BABY JESUS

Read Luke 2 v 22-38

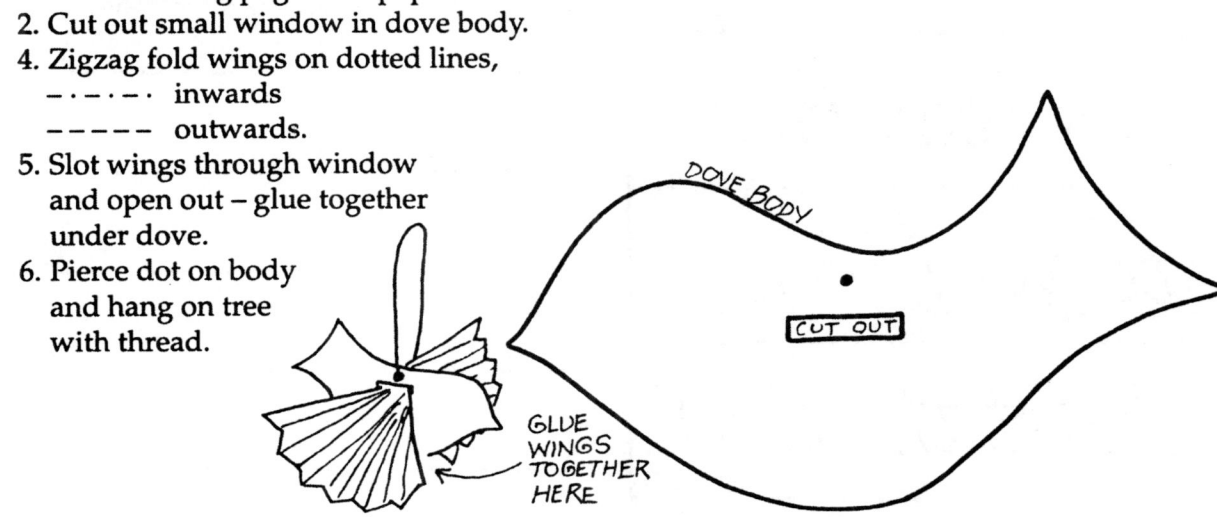

35A. EXPANDING ANGEL DECORATION

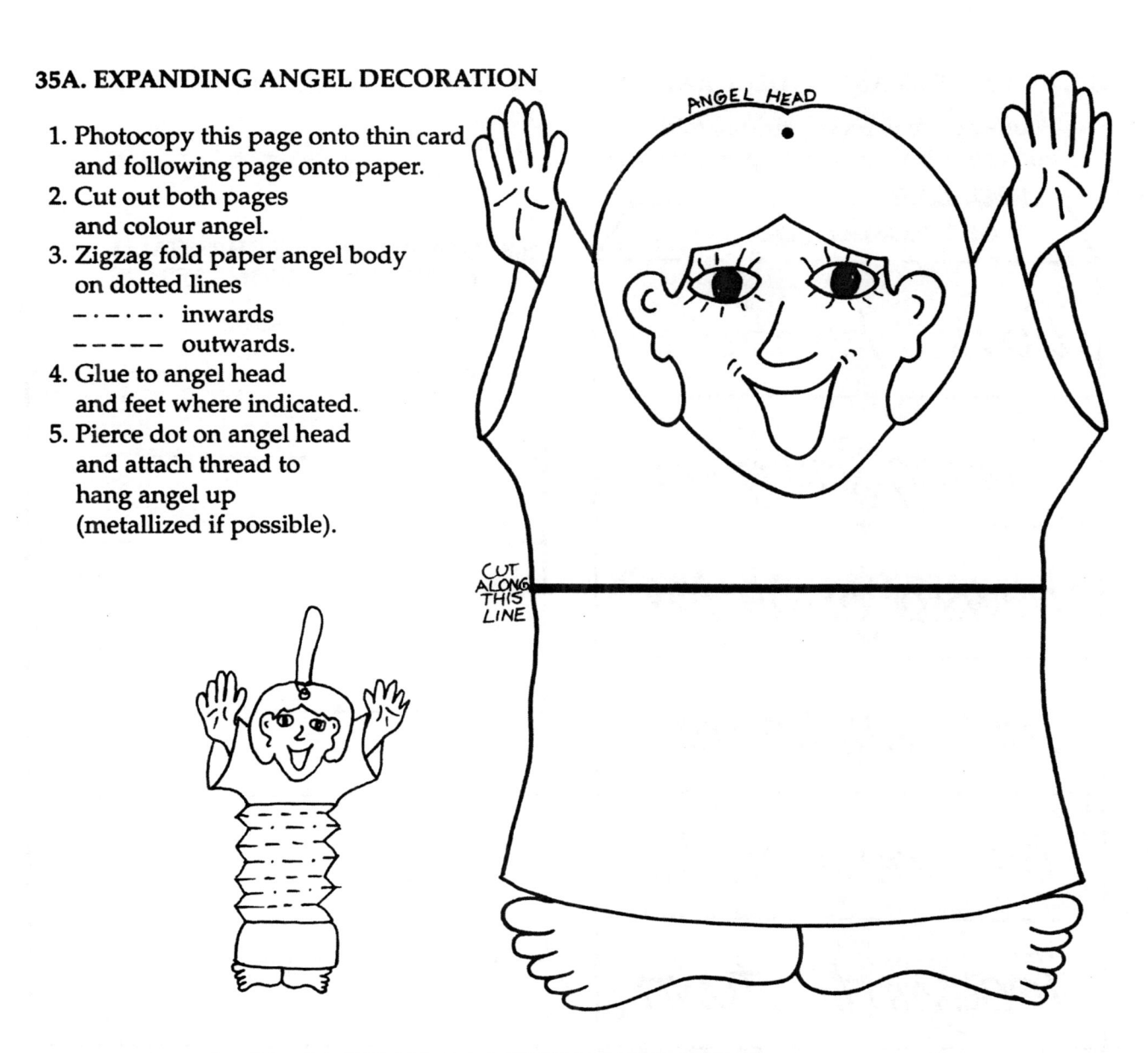

1. Photocopy this page onto thin card and following page onto paper.
2. Cut out both pages and colour angel.
3. Zigzag fold paper angel body on dotted lines
   - –·–·– inwards
   - – – – – outwards.
4. Glue to angel head and feet where indicated.
5. Pierce dot on angel head and attach thread to hang angel up (metallized if possible).

ANGEL HEAD

CUT ALONG THIS LINE

35B. DOVE OF PEACE CHRISTMAS TREE DECORATION

1. Photocopy this page onto thin card and following page onto paper.
2. Cut out small window in dove body.
4. Zigzag fold wings on dotted lines,
   - –·–·– inwards
   - – – – – outwards.
5. Slot wings through window and open out – glue together under dove.
6. Pierce dot on body and hang on tree with thread.

DOVE BODY

CUT OUT

GLUE WINGS TOGETHER HERE

36A. EXPANDING ANGEL DECORATION – BODY

Photocopy onto **paper**, zig-zag fold and use as instructions on previous page.

ANGEL BODY

GLUE TO ANGEL HEAD

"Do not be afraid.

I bring you good

news of great joy

that will be for

all the people.

Today in the town

of David a Saviour

has been born

to you; he is

Christ the Lord."

GLUE TO ANGEL FEET

36B. DOVE OF PEACE CHRISTMAS TREE DECORATION – WINGS

Photocopy onto paper.

DOVE WINGS

37. CHRISTMAS MOBILE – STABLE ROOF

1. Photocopy this page and following two pages onto thin card.
2. Colour in and cut out all pieces.
3. Glue front and back together for all pieces except star and pierce dots at top for hanging.
4. For star, fold all three pieces inwards on dotted lines and glue all three together to form three-dimensional star. Pierce dots at top and points.
5. Pierce all dots on stable roof, then glue on tab as marked to form roof shape.
6. Attach thread to top of star for hanging up – attach points X, Y, Z to pairs of holes X, Y, Z on stable roof to hang approx. 12cm from roof.
7. Hang figures by threads from appropriate dot i.e. Mary from A etc. Use **hanging** lengths of thread as indicated beside figures – allow extra for tying.

CUT OUT CIRCLE

GLUE ROOF TOGETHER HERE

38. CHRISTMAS MOBILE – STAR, BABY JESUS, ANIMALS

COW
26 CM
THREAD

BABY JESUS
7CM
THREAD

DONKEY
26 CM
THREAD

39. CHRISTMAS MOBILE – MARY, JOSEPH, KING, SHEPHERD

MARY 7CM THREAD

JOSEPH 7CM THREAD

KING 17CM THREAD

SHEPHERD 17CM THREAD

40. SHEEP FACE BASEBALL CAP

1. Enlarge A4 to A3 size – most photocopiers have a setting for this.
2. Photocopy onto paper or, better still, thin card if you can obtain this in A3 card.
3. Cut slits on parallel lines on top of cap.
4. Cut out cap and ears – colour ears black and staple onto marked spots.
5. Staple AB to CD at back, overlapping to give a good fit.
6. You could use the sheep caps to act out a Christmas play with sheep in it.

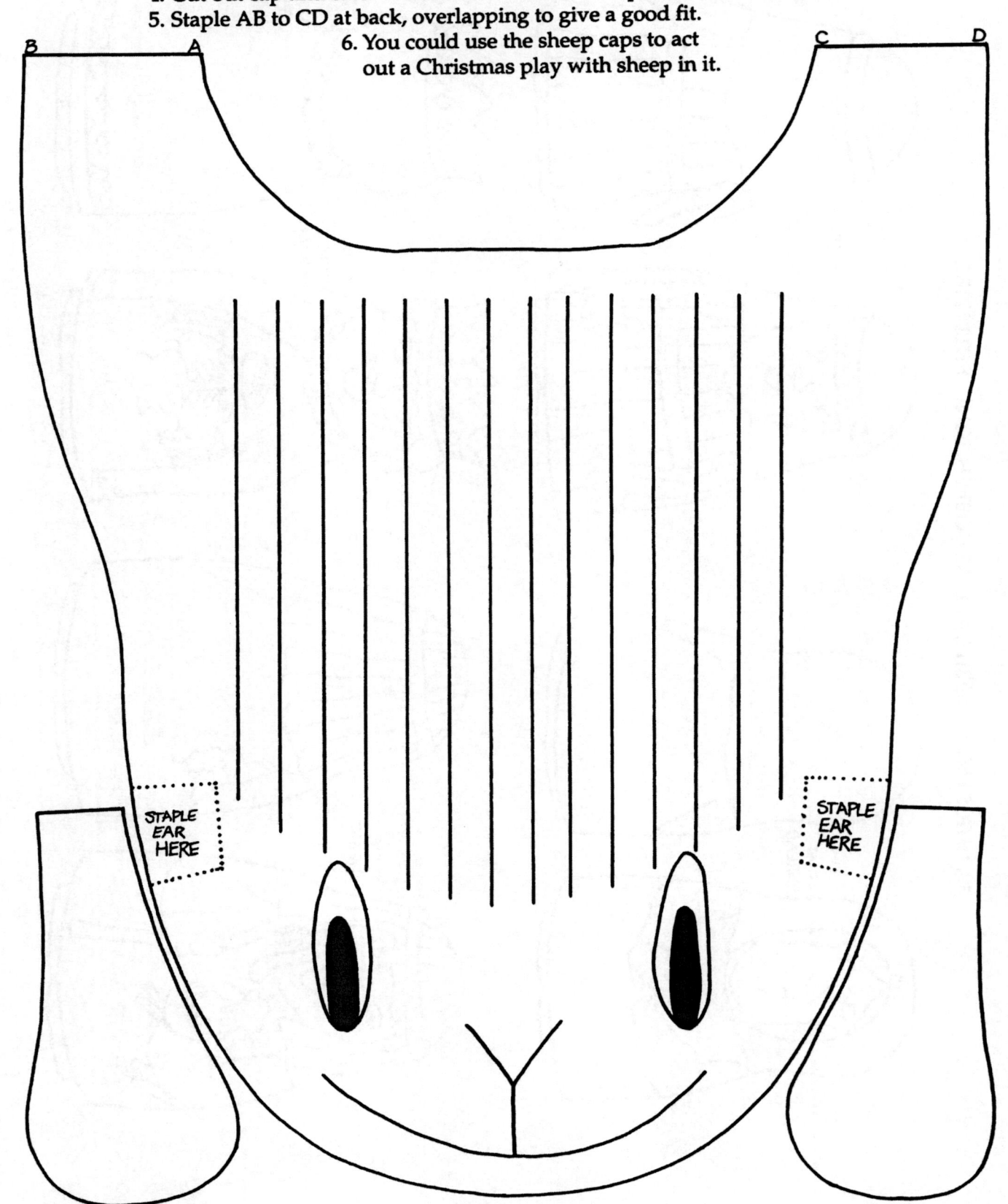

41. CHRISTMAS WINDOW PICTURE

1. Photocopy onto TRACING PAPER – use good quality tracing paper, obtainable from art/stationers shops, in A4 size – this should be hand fed through the photocopier.
2. Colour using felt-tip pens for translucent effect.
3. Stick to a window using sticky putty.

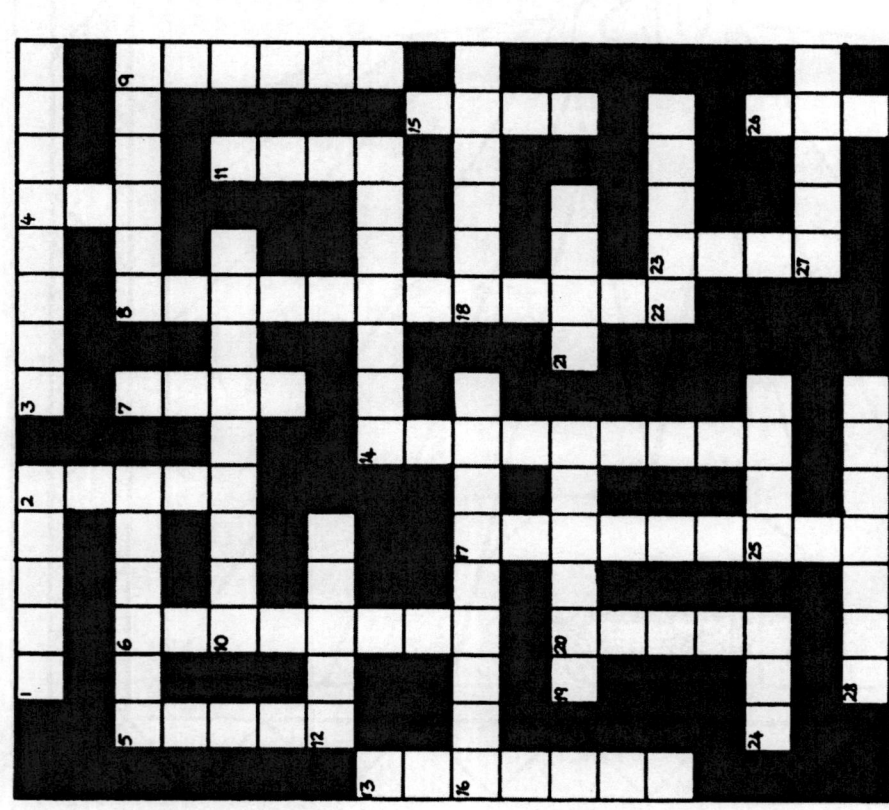

42. CHRISTMAS CROSSWORD

ACROSS

1. God's way of warning the wise men (5)
3. The angel brought the shepherds good news of this for all people (5,3)
5. Not a very smart crib (6)
8. Watched by shepherds at night (6)
10. Saw an angel while burning incense in the temple (9)
12. Wanted to kill baby Jesus (5)
14. Jesus means this (7)
16. Jesus' birthplace (9)
18. Caesar Augustus decreed it should be taken (6)
19. He prophesied that a virgin would give birth to a son called Immanuel (6)
21. Widow of eighty-four who never left the temple (4)
22. Place to escape from Herod (5)
24. Number 21 was definitely very this (3)
25. Wise men came from here (4)
27. Joseph belonged to the house and line of this king (5)
28. Angels said, 'Glory to God in the . . . . ' (7)

DOWN

2. A sweet-smelling gift (5)
4. Boys under this age were not safe in Bethlehem (3)
5. He prophesied where Jesus would be born (5)
6. Mary and Joseph travelled from here to Bethlehem (8)
7. Gabriel announced Jesus' birth to her (4)
8. A gift from far away (12)
9. Told by the Holy Spirit he would not die until he had seen the Christ (6)
11. Followed to the baby by foreign visitors (4)
13. He announced the birth of John of Zechariah to Zechariah (7)
14. First visitors to the baby Jesus (9)
15. For not believing, Zechariah was this until his son was born (4)
17. Mother of John (9)
20. Simeon told Mary that this would pierce her own soul (5)
23. A kingly gift (4)
26. The number of months that John was older than Jesus (3)

(If you need help finding the answers have a look in Matthew Chapters 1 and 2, and Luke Chapters 1 and 2.)

43. CHRISTMAS PUZZLE PAGE

Help Mary and Joseph to escape to Egypt through the maze

DECODE THIS VERSE to find out something the angel Gabriel told Mary about Jesus. Move each letter one place forward in the alphabet: a=b, b=c, c=d, z=a, etc.

gd vhkk qdhfm nudq sgd gntrd ne izbna

__ ____ _____ ____ ___ _____ __ _____

enq dudq ghr jhmfcnl vhkk mdudq dmc

___ ____ ___ _____ ____ _____ ___

STABLE JIGSAW – Match the pieces to those on the stable. Write on the words to find out what the angels told the shepherds.

WORDSEARCH – See how many names of people and places in the Christmas story you can find – there are 14 altogether. (forwards, backwards, up, down, diagonally.)

A	N	N	A	Z	M	A	R	N	A
Z	E	C	A	J	E	G	Y	P	T
M	E	S	E	Z	L	E	J	E	H
E	S	C	L	R	A	J	O	O	D
H	U	X	H	R	S	R	S	J	O
E	S	N	J	A	U	M	E	S	R
L	E	O	H	E	R	O	P	T	E
H	J	E	Y	O	E	I	H	L	H
T	E	M	A	R	J	M	A	R	Y
E	L	I	Z	A	B	E	T	H	O
B	H	S	L	E	I	R	B	A	G

44. ADVENT CALENDAR – PART ONE: FRONT

1. Photocopy this **and following** page onto thin card.
2. NB **before** session with children, adult must cut the doors with craft knife: cut round 3 sides (or curve) on solid lines only – do not fold back at this stage. (Instructions continue on page 45.)

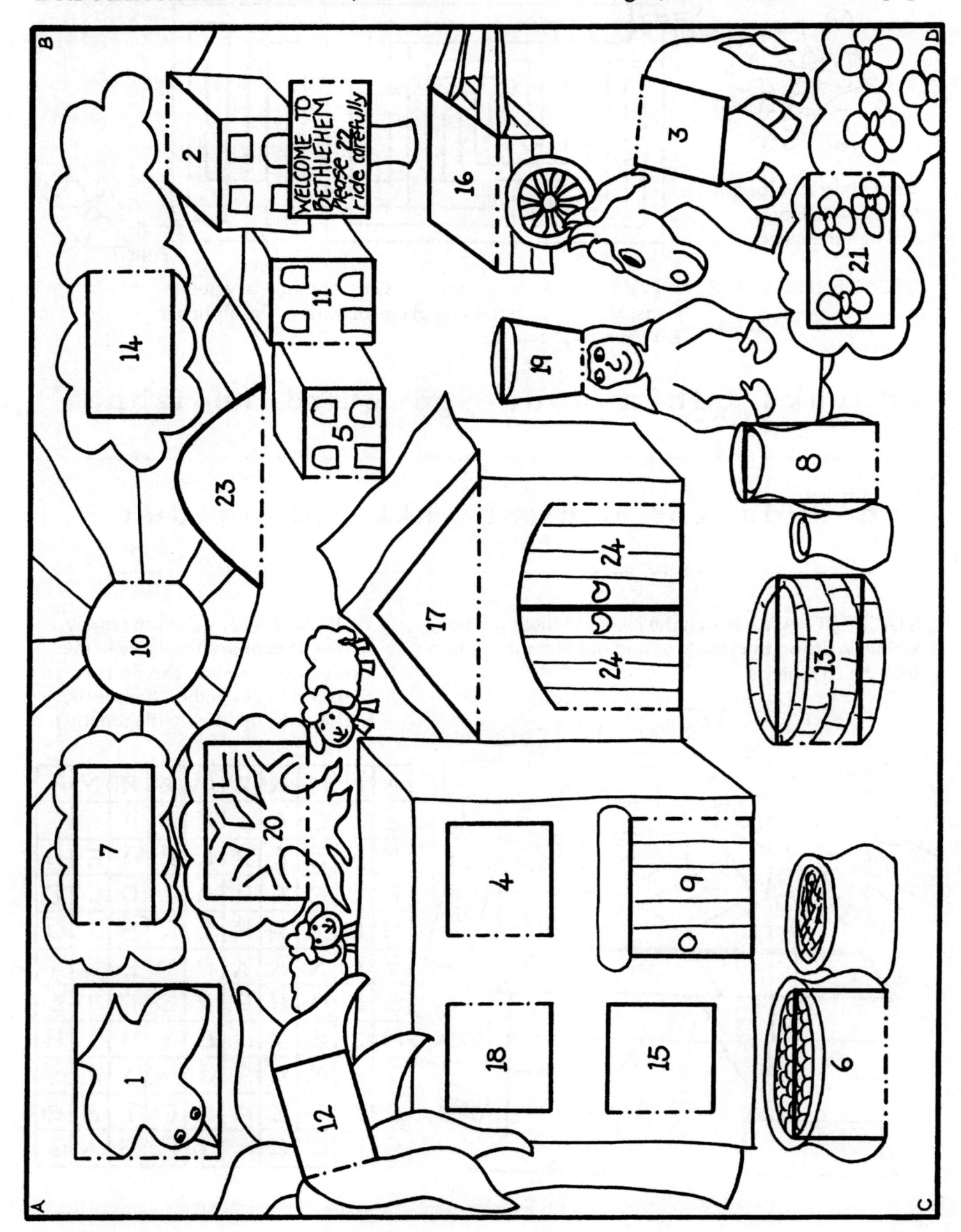

45. ADVENT CALENDAR – PART TWO: BACK

Instructions continued: 3. Cut round outer edge front and back. 4. Colour in both pieces. 5. Glue thin strip round edge of back as marked – place front on top, lining up edges **carefully**, with corners A, B, C, D over A, B, C, D on back.

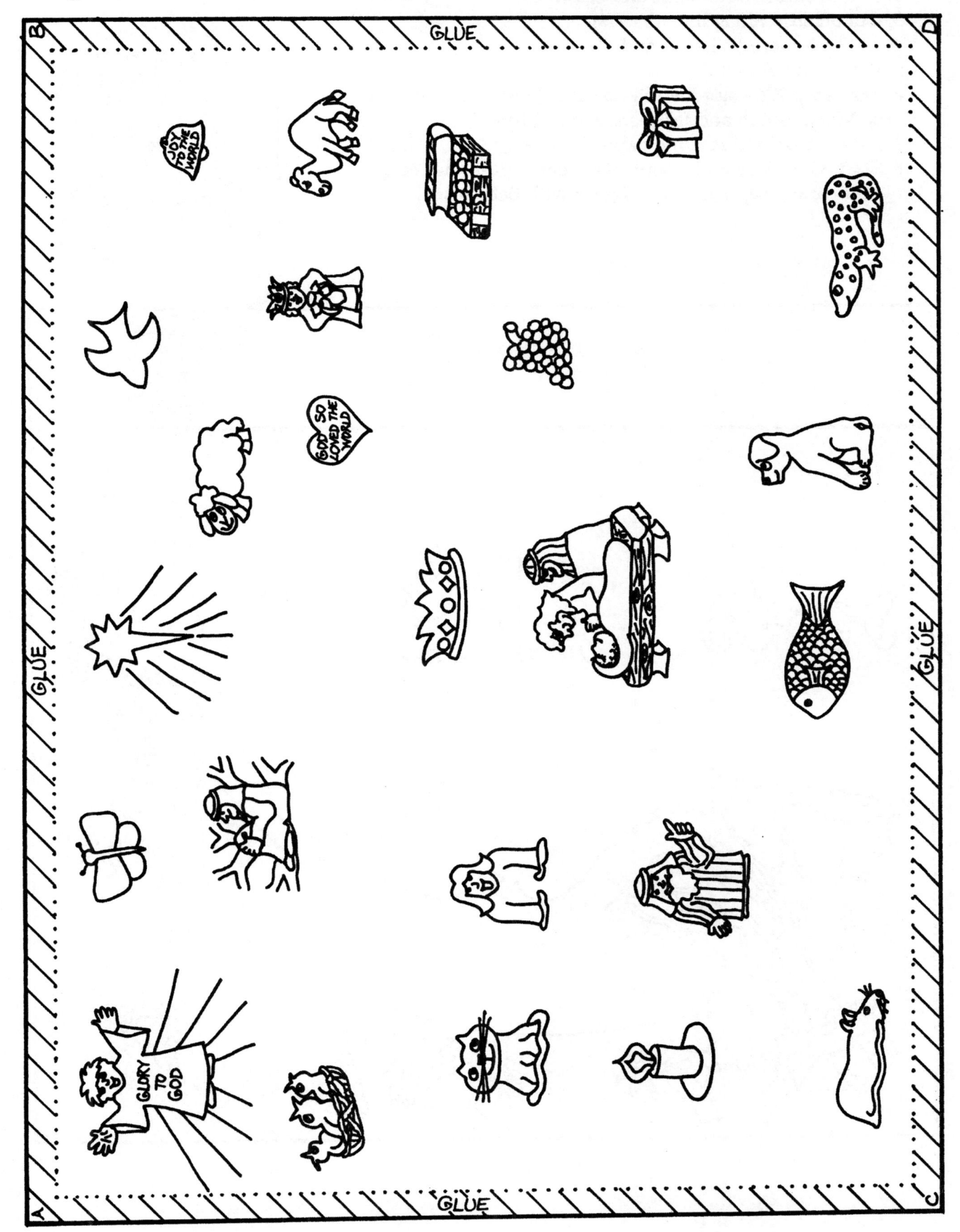

46. FLIGHT INTO EGYPT – ACTION MODEL

1. Photocopy onto thin card.
2. Colour round outer edge and colour in.
3. Cut off strip along line XY.
4. Cut two curved slits PQ and RS.
5. Pierce dots A and B.
6. Take strip XY – slot X end into slit PQ and Y end into slit RS, so Mary, Joseph and Jesus show on picture.
7. Attach B behind A using paper fastener.
8. Start with Mary and Joseph at QS end – pull X to make Mary and Joseph escape to Egypt with Baby Jesus.

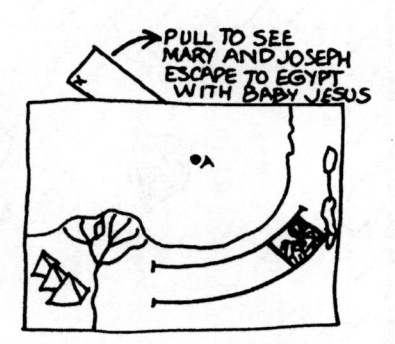

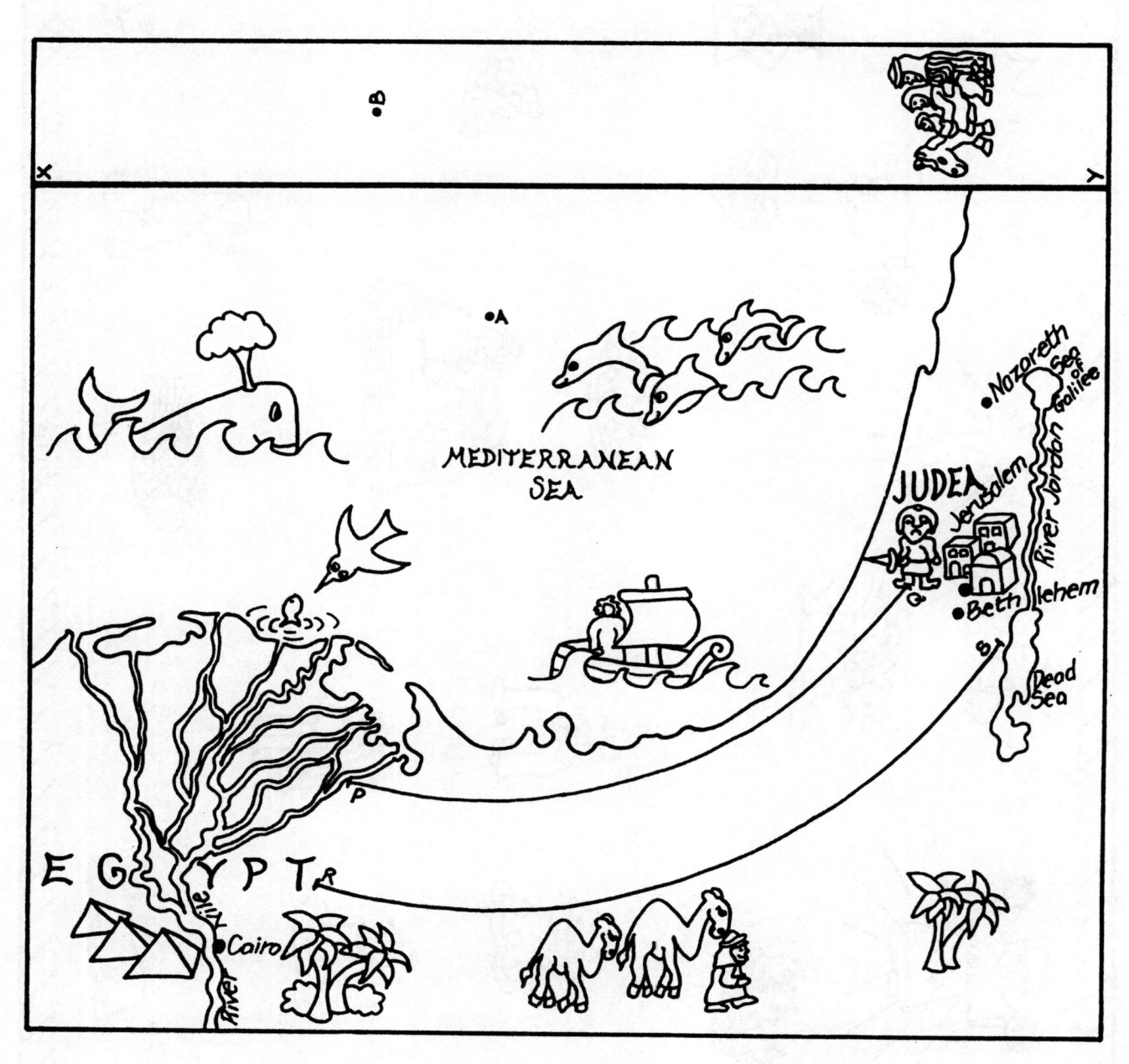

47. FOLD-OUT CRIB SCENE – JOSEPH

1. Photocopy this and following 8 pages onto thin card.
2. Colour and cut out. Fold all foldlines – score first.
3. Cut out inner outlines on pages 1, 2, 4, 5, 7 and 8 so that there is a window in the centre.
4. Glue Baby Jesus to main piece from page 2.
5. Glue piece 1 to piece 2 on marked tabs.
6. Then glue piece 1/2 to piece 3.
7. Glue pieces 4, 5, 6 together and 7, 8, 9 together.
8. Glue 'shepherd' section on left hand side of stable and 'wise men' section on right hand side of stable section, as shown in diagram.

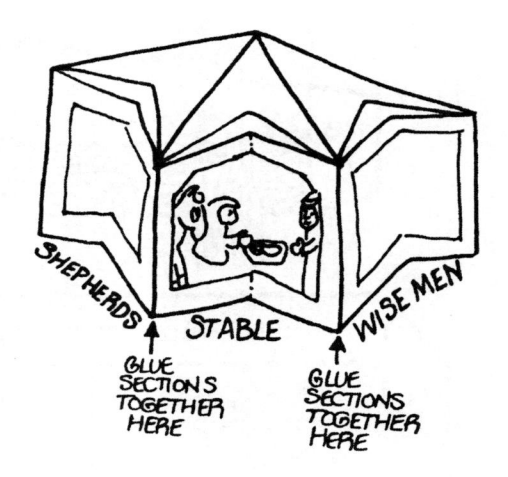

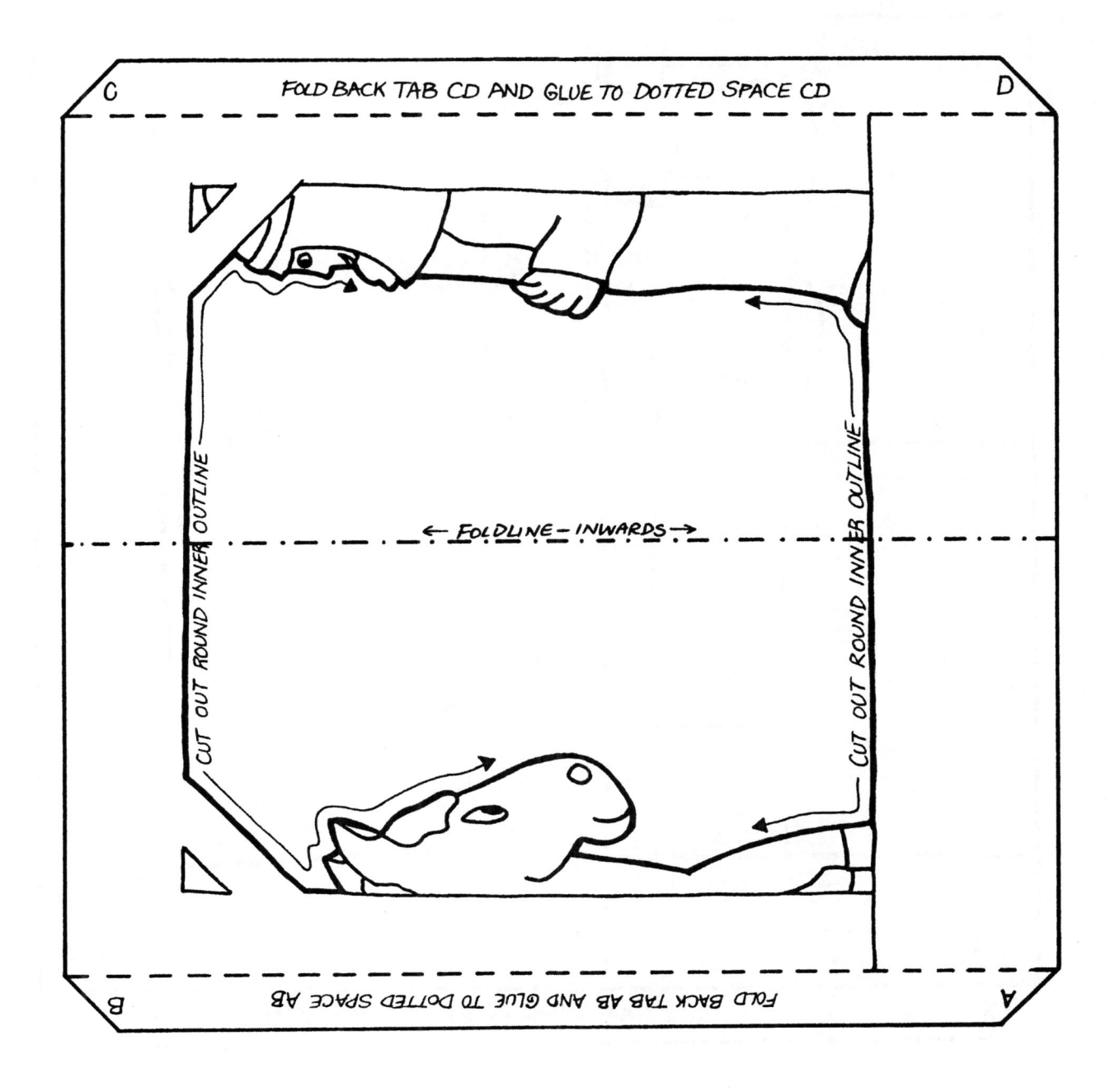

48. FOLD-OUT CRIB SCENE – MARY AND BABY JESUS

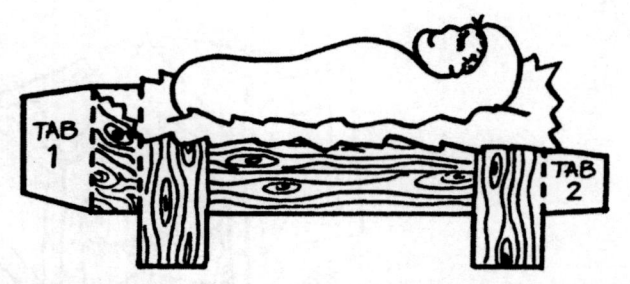

TAB 1

TAB 2

Y — FOLD BACK – GLUE TO SPACE YZ — Z

A — GLUE TAB AB HERE — B

CUT ROUND INNER OUTLINE

CUT ROUND INNER OUTLINE

← FOLD INWARDS →

D — GLUE TAB CD HERE — C

X — FOLD BACK – GLUE TO SPACE WX — W

49. FOLD-OUT CRIB SCENE – STABLE

W · — GLUE TAB WX HERE — · X

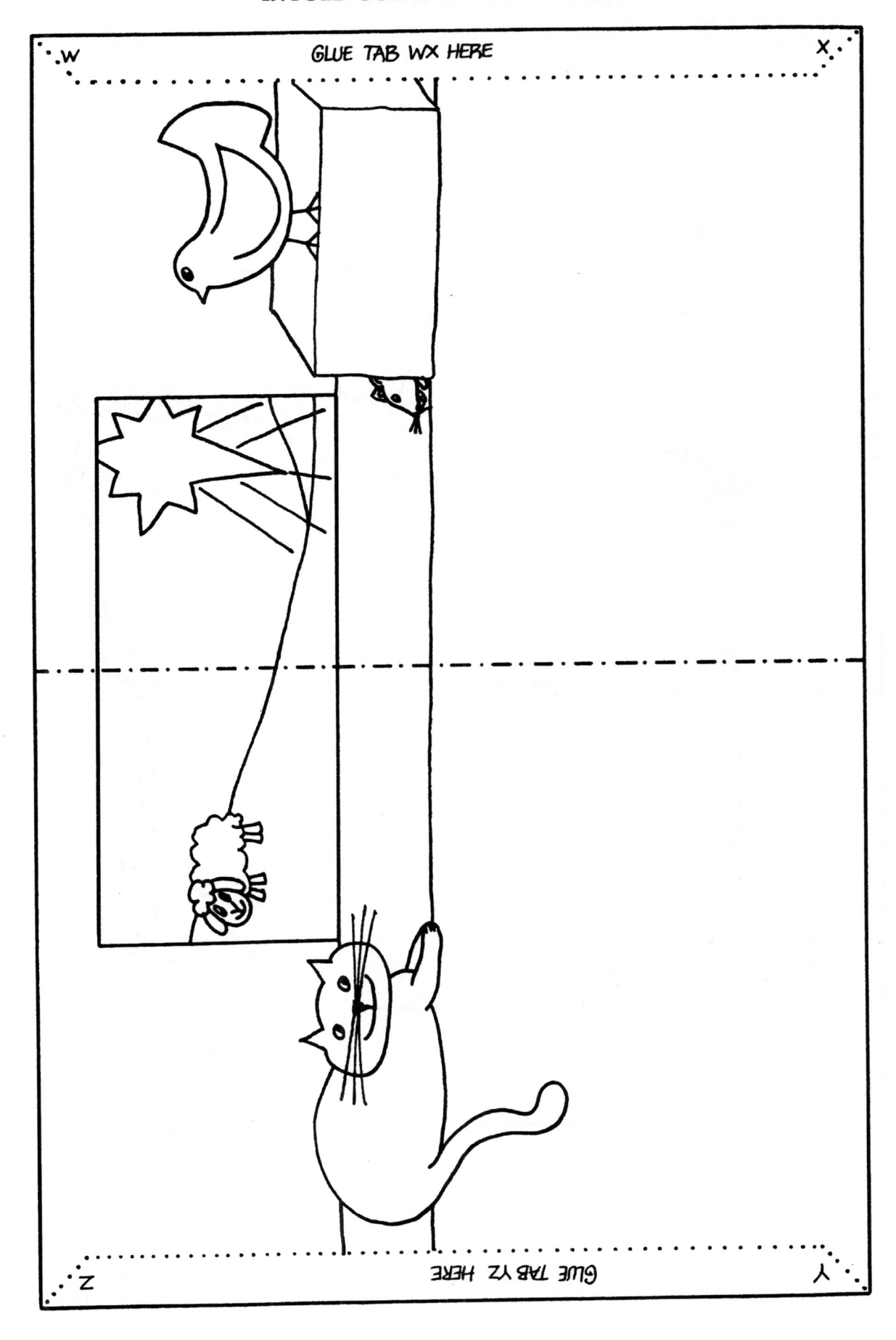

Z · — GLUE TAB YZ HERE — · Y

50. FOLD-OUT CRIB SCENE – SHEPHERDS

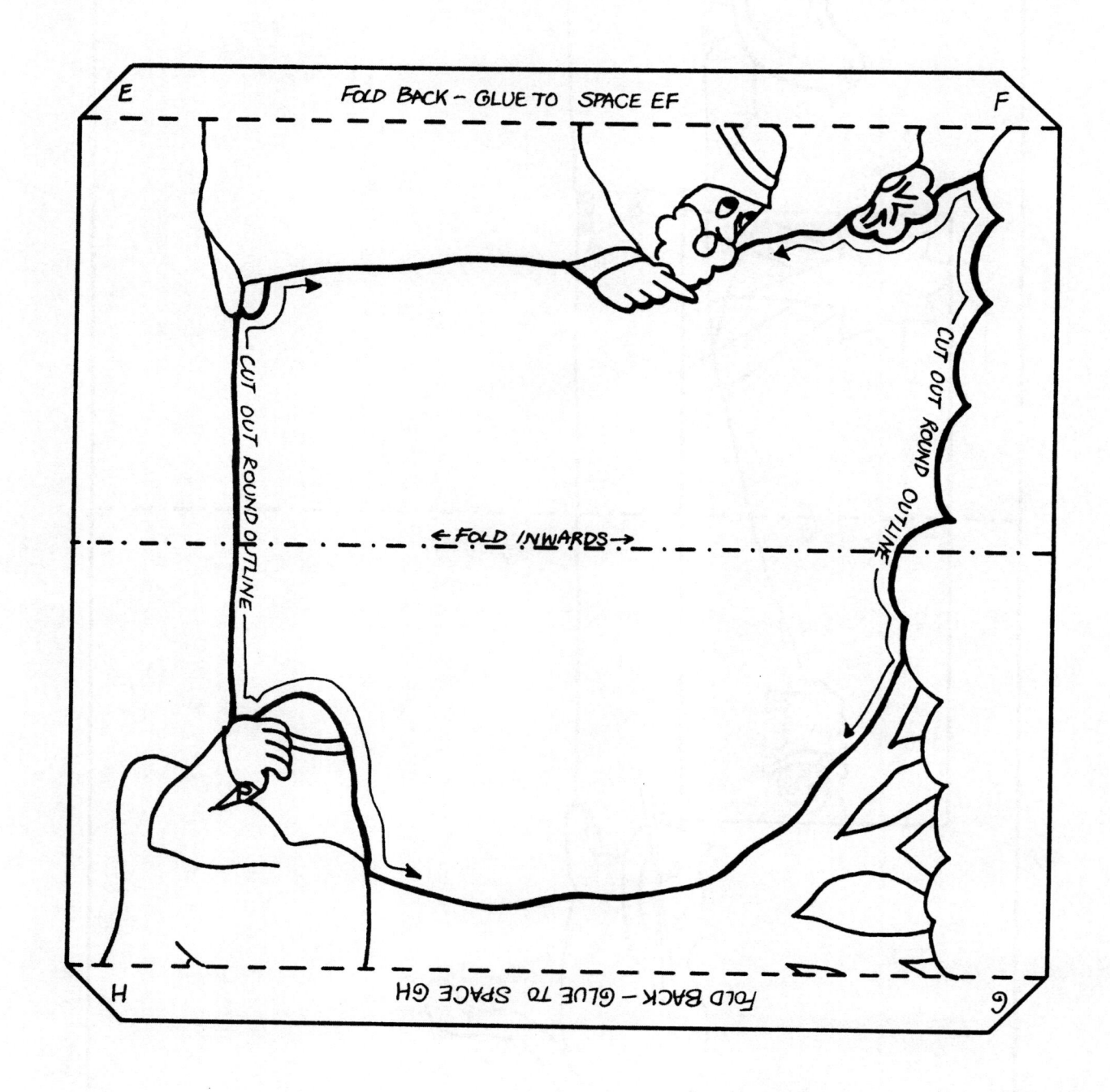

51. FOLD-OUT CRIB SCENE – ANGELS

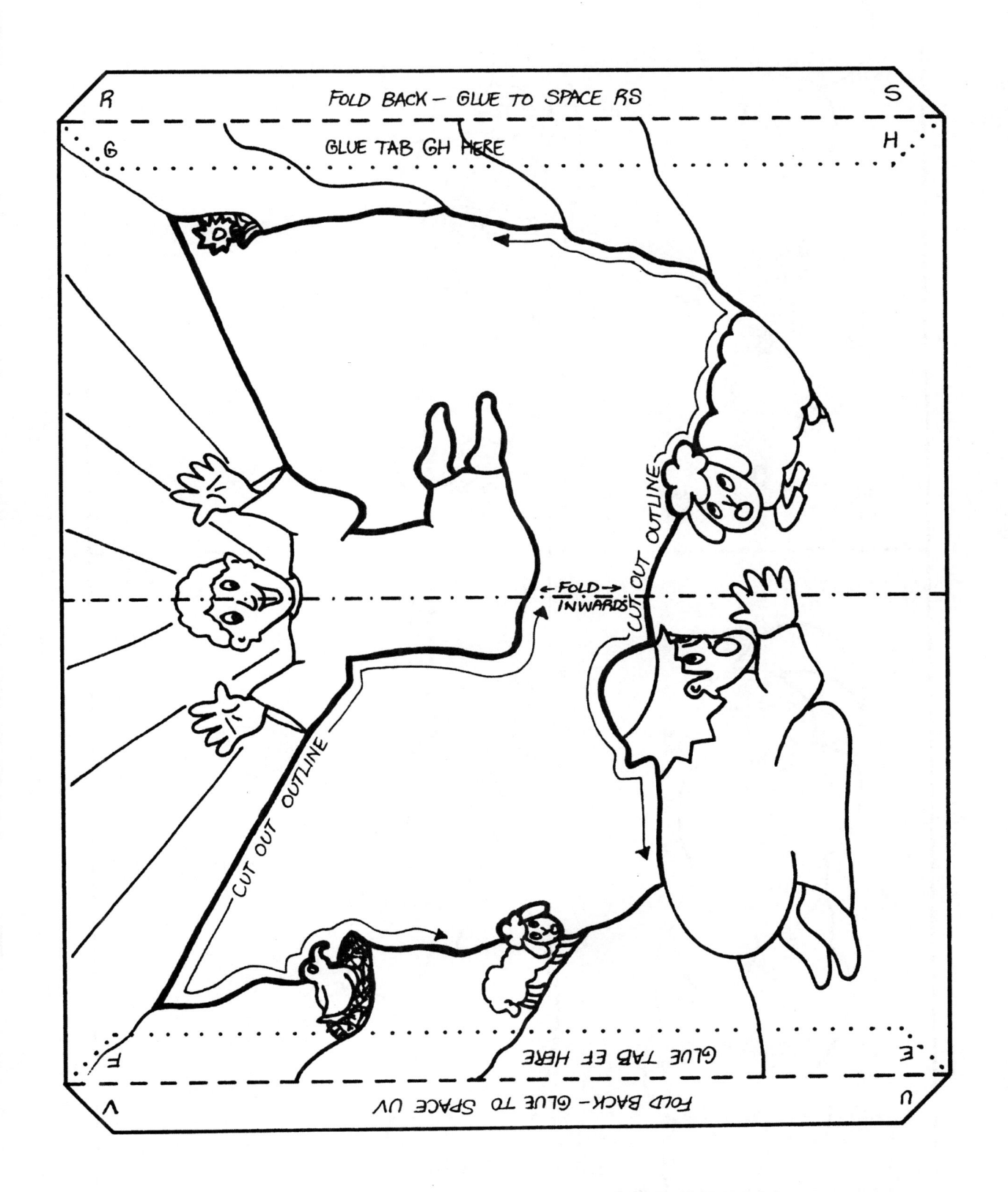

52. FOLD-OUT CRIB SCENE – FIELDS

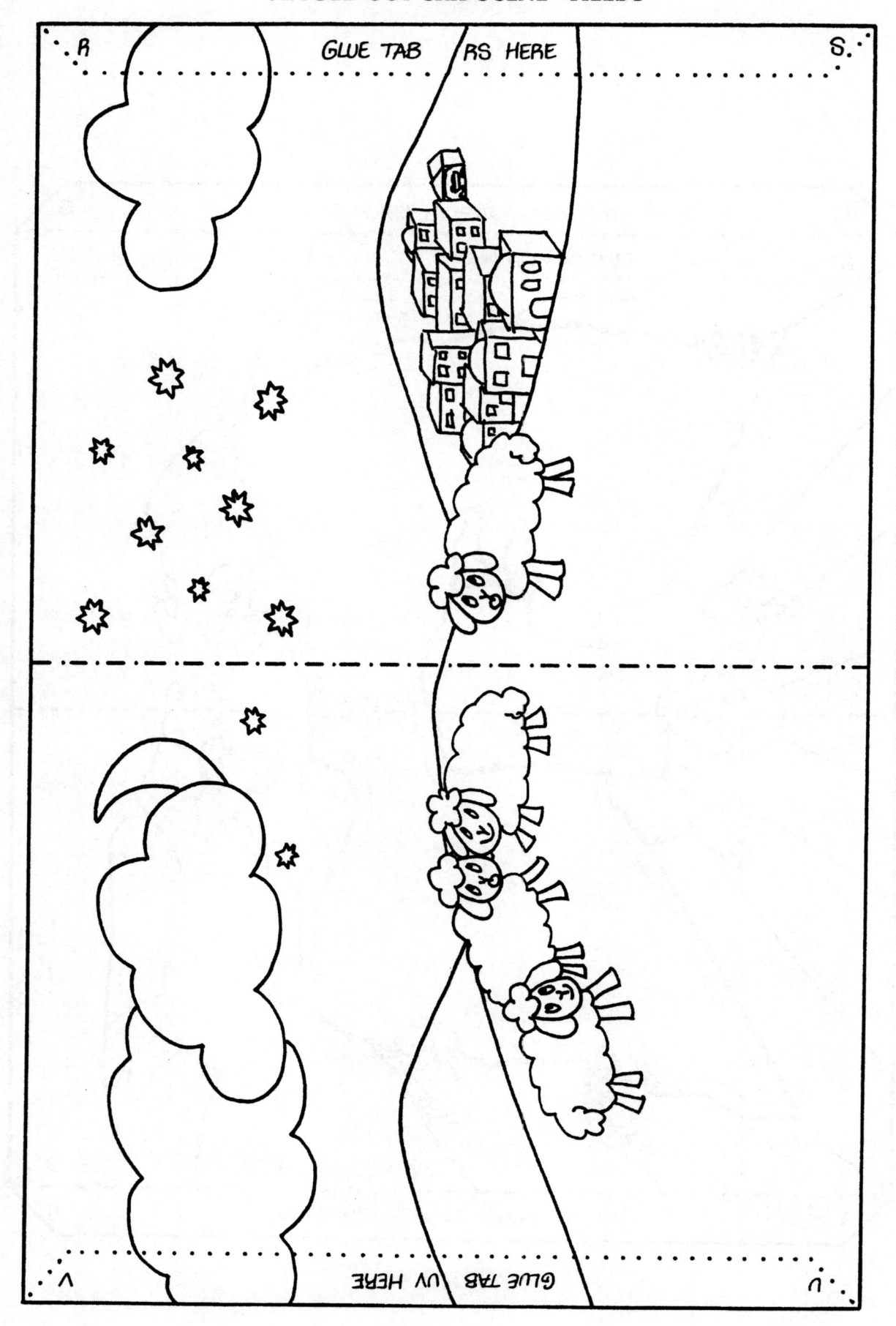

53. FOLD-OUT CRIB SCENE – WISE MAN 1

54. FOLD-OUT CRIB SCENE – WISE MEN 2 AND 3

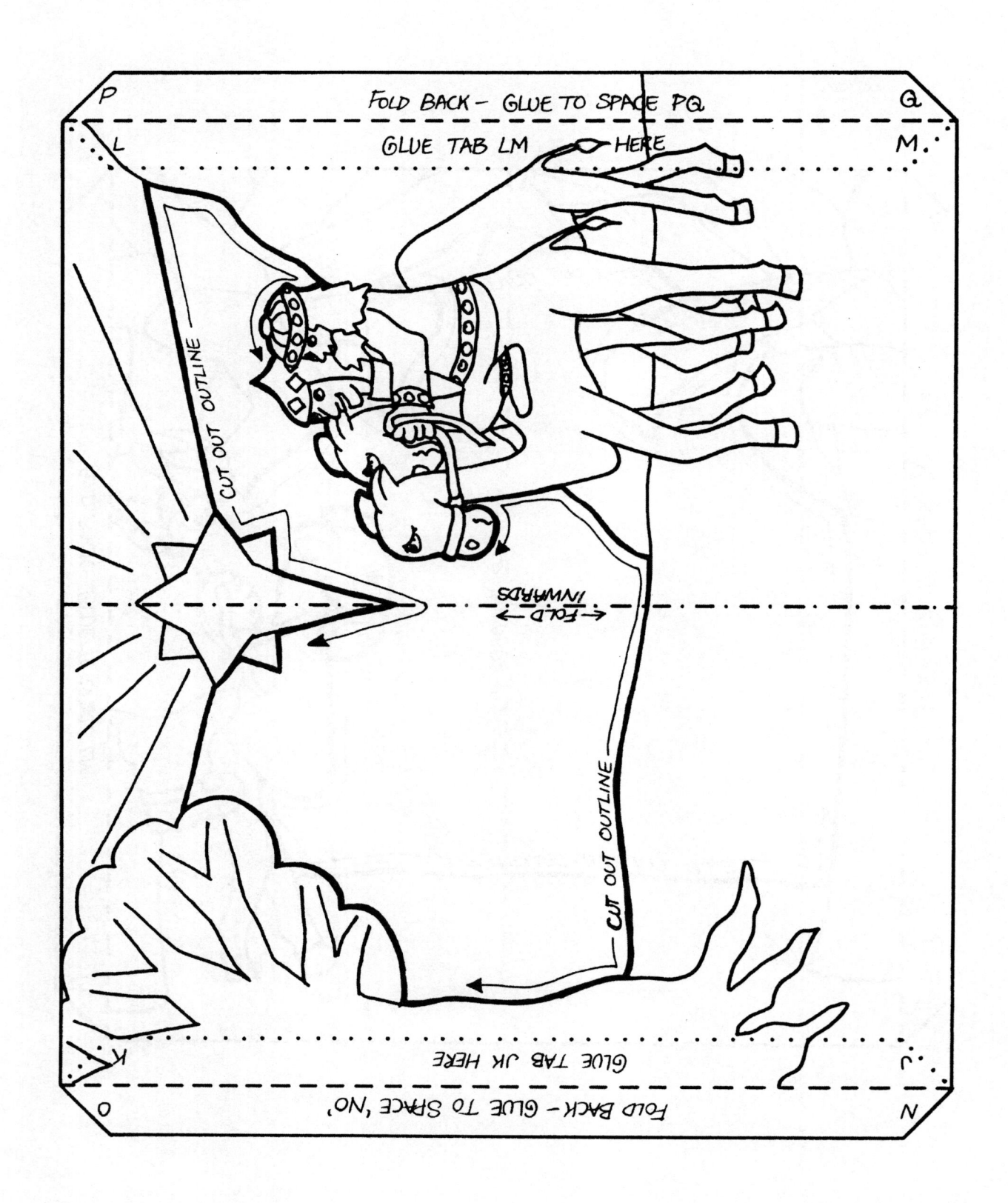

55. FOLD-OUT CRIB SCENE – BETHLEHEM

GLUE TAB PQ HERE

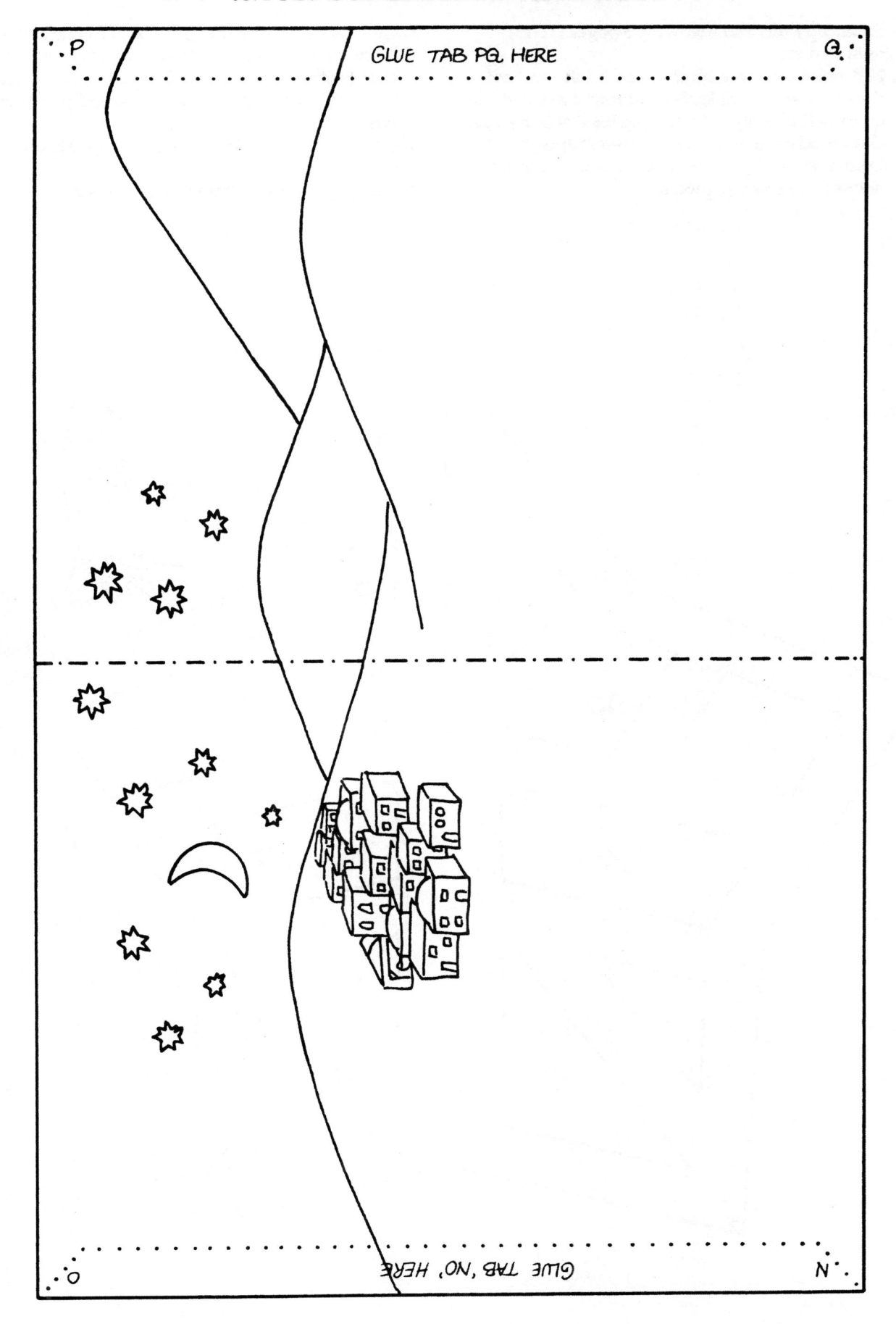

GLUE TAB 'NO' HERE

56. 3-D STAR ADVENT CALENDAR MOBILE – PART ONE

1. Photocopy this and following 3 pages (11-13) onto thin card.
2. N.B. *before* session with children, adult must cut the doors with craft knife – cut round 2 or 3 sides on solid lines only – do not fold back at this stage.
3. Cut round outer edges of all 4 star shapes.
4. Colour in small pictures. Colour doors or draw pattern on front star pieces.
5. Glue thin strip round edge of back as marked – place top stars (with doors) on top of correct back stars (with pictures) – matching up A, B, C points and XYZ points and line up edges and points *very* carefully.
6. Cut slits AD and VW and slot two stars together at right angles.
7. Hang up by taping thread to A top point.

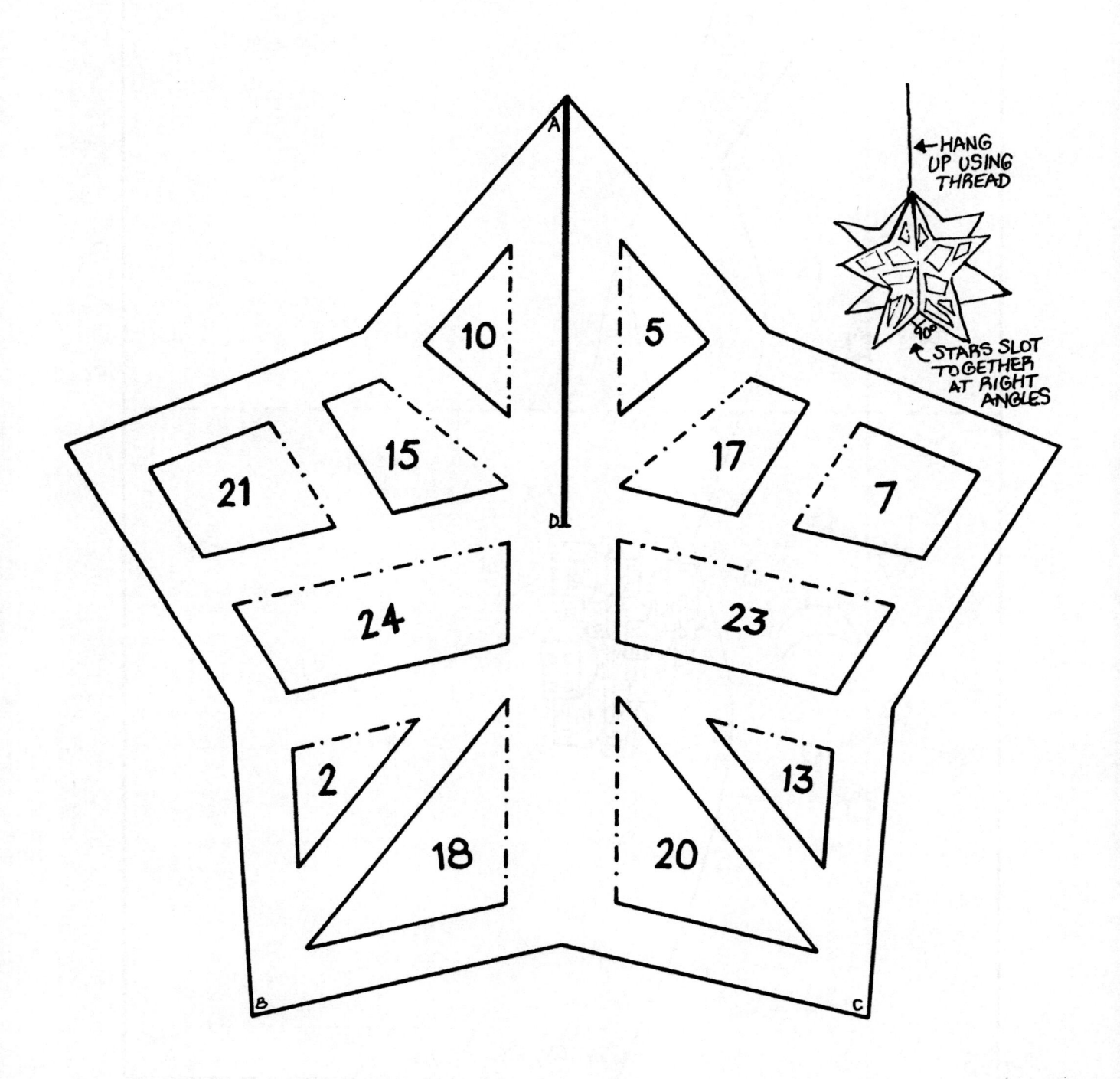

57. 3-D STAR ADVENT CALENDAR MOBILE – PART TWO

58. 3-D STAR ADVENT CALENDAR MOBILE – PART THREE

59. 3-D STAR ADVENT CALENDAR MOBILE – PART FOUR

60. ADVENT ACTION 1

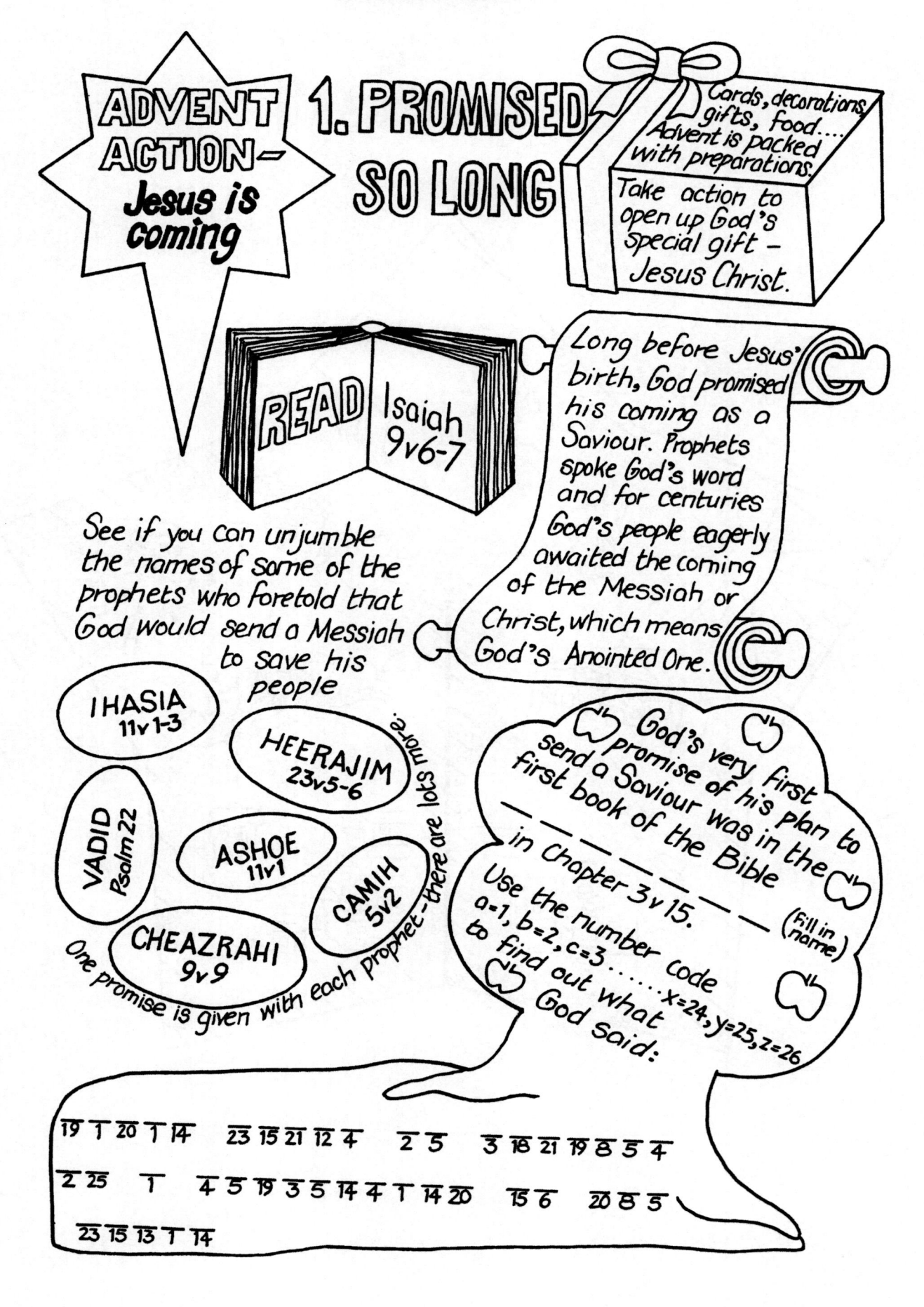

ADVENT ACTION — Jesus is coming

1. PROMISED SO LONG

Cards, decorations, gifts, food.... Advent is packed with preparations. Take action to open up God's special gift — Jesus Christ.

READ Isaiah 9v6-7

Long before Jesus' birth, God promised his coming as a Saviour. Prophets spoke God's word and for centuries God's people eagerly awaited the coming of the Messiah or Christ, which means God's Anointed One.

See if you can unjumble the names of some of the prophets who foretold that God would send a Messiah to save his people

- IHASIA 11v1-3
- HEERAJIM 23v5-6
- VADID Psalm 22
- ASHOE 11v1
- CAMIH 5v2
- CHEAZRAHI 9v9

One promise is given with each prophet — there are lots more.

God's very first promise of his plan to send a Saviour was in the first book of the Bible _____ (fill in name) in Chapter 3 v 15.

Use the number code a=1, b=2, c=3 ...... x=24, y=25, z=26 to find out what God said:

19 T 20 T 14   23 15 21 12 4   2 5   3 18 21 19 8 5 4

2 25   T   4 5 19 3 5 14 4 T 14 20   15 6   20 8 5

23 15 13 T 14

61. ADVENT ACTION 2

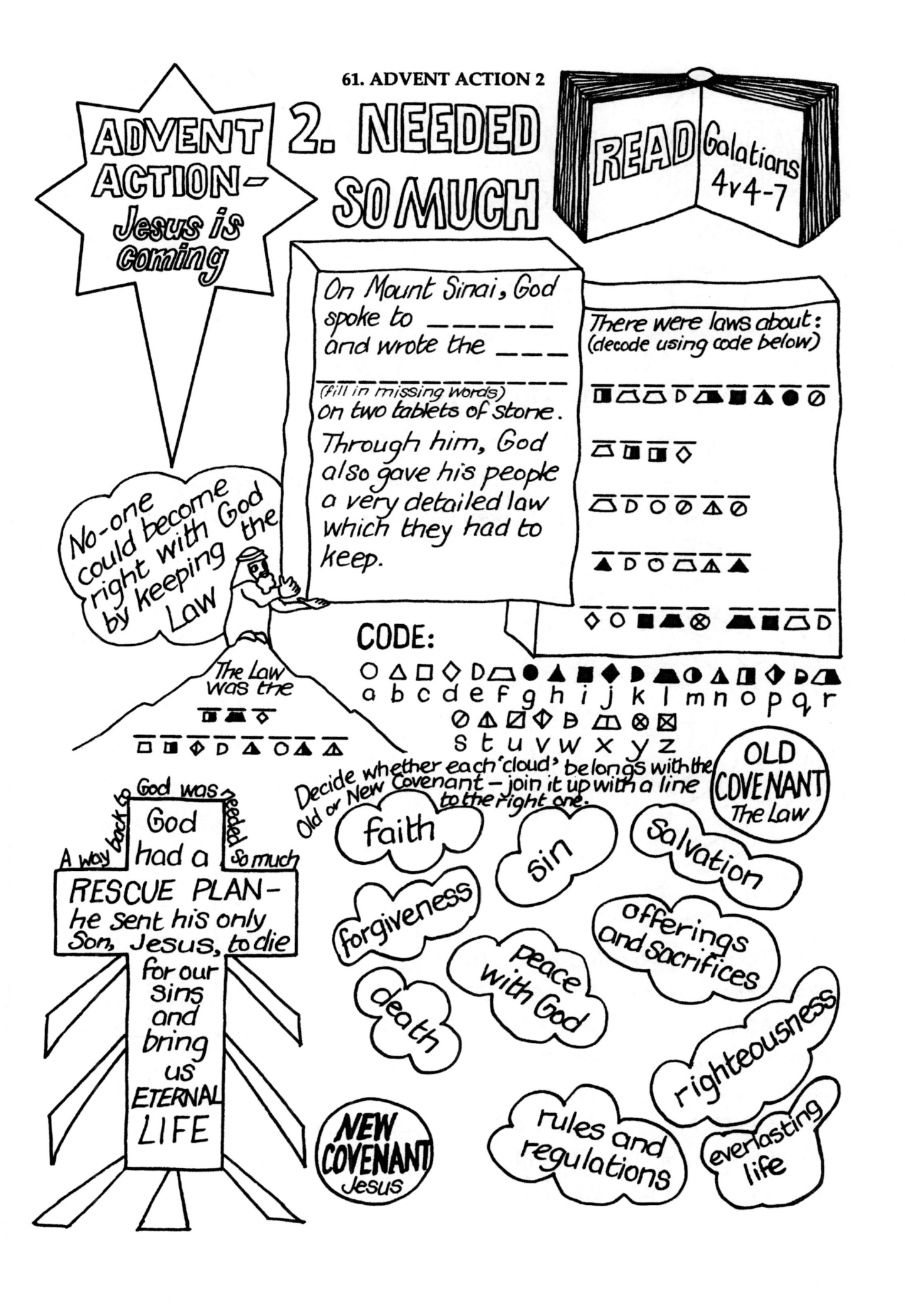

ADVENT ACTION – Jesus is coming
2. NEEDED SO MUCH

READ Galatians 4 v 4-7

On Mount Sinai, God spoke to _____ and wrote the ___ ___ ___ _____ (fill in missing words) on two tablets of stone. Through him, God also gave his people a very detailed law which they had to keep.

There were laws about: (decode using code below)

- ☐ ⌂ ☐ D ⌂ ▲ ● ⌀
- ⌂ ▪ ☐ ◇
- ⌂ D ⊘ ⌂ ◯
- ▲ D ◯ ⌂ ▲
- ◇ ◯ ▪ ⌂ ⊗ ▲ ▪ ⌂ D

CODE:
O △ □ ◇ D ⌂ ● ▲ ■ ◐ ▲ ◯ △ ▫ ◇ ▶ ⌂
a b c d e f g h i j k l m n o p q r
⊘ ⌂ ⌂ ▽ ⌧ B ⌂ ⊗ ⊠
s t u v w x y z

"No-one could become right with God by keeping the Law"

The Law was the ☐ ▪ ◇ / □ ☐ ◇ D ⌂ ▲ ◯ ⌂ ⌂

Decide whether each 'cloud' belongs with the Old or New Covenant — join it up with a line to the right one.

OLD COVENANT – The Law

NEW COVENANT – Jesus

Clouds: faith, sin, salvation, forgiveness, offerings and sacrifices, death, peace with God, righteousness, rules and regulations, everlasting life

A way back to God was needed so much

God had a RESCUE PLAN – he sent his only Son, Jesus, to die for our sins and bring us ETERNAL LIFE

62. ADVENT ACTION 3

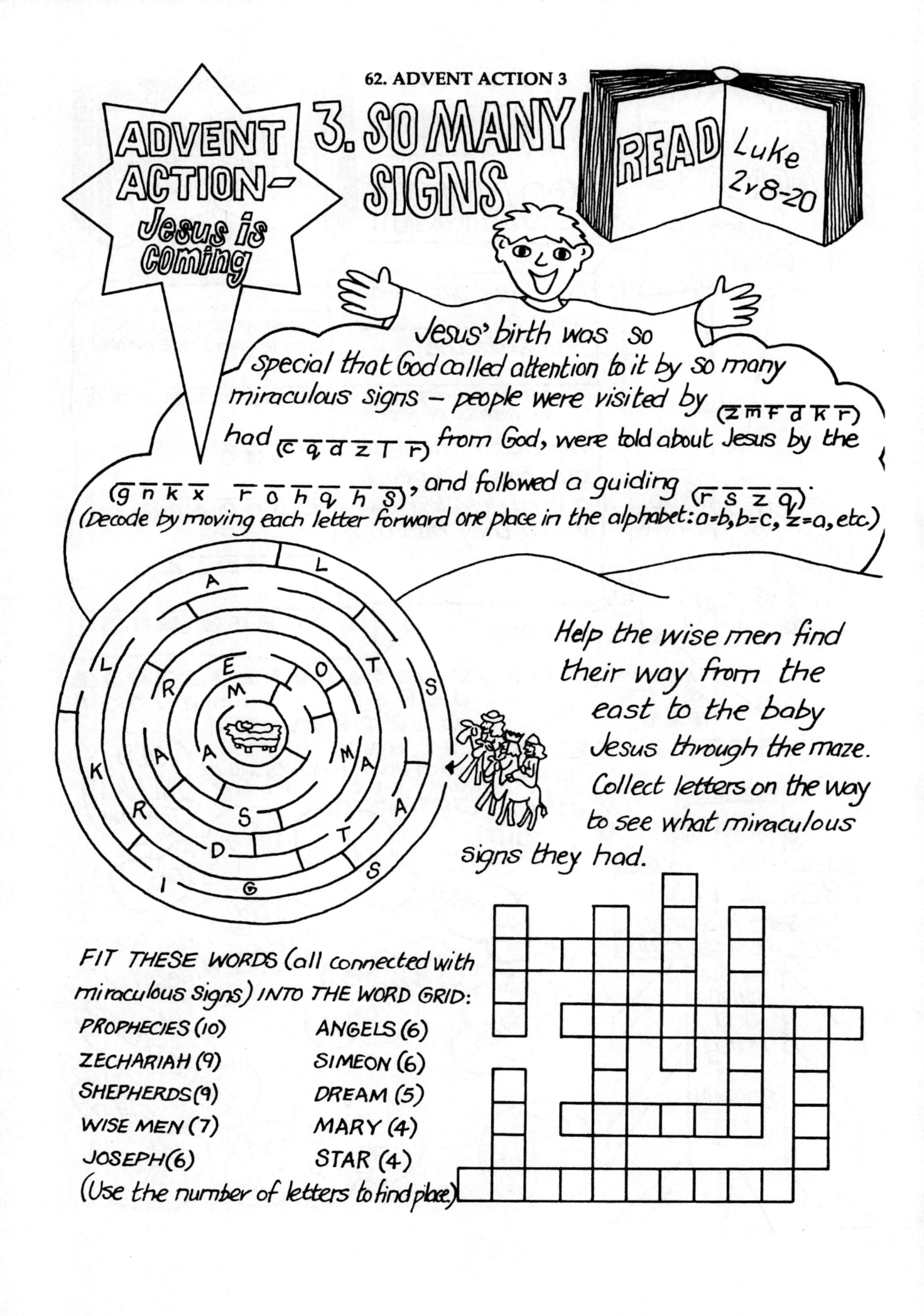

ADVENT ACTION - Jesus is coming
3. SO MANY SIGNS

READ Luke 2 v 8-20

Jesus' birth was so special that God called attention to it by so many miraculous signs – people were visited by (zmfdkr) had (cqdzTr) from God, were told about Jesus by the (gnkx rohqhs), and followed a guiding (rszq).
(Decode by moving each letter forward one place in the alphabet: a=b, b=c, z=a, etc.)

Help the wise men find their way from the east to the baby Jesus through the maze. Collect letters on the way to see what miraculous signs they had.

FIT THESE WORDS (all connected with miraculous signs) INTO THE WORD GRID:

- PROPHECIES (10)
- ZECHARIAH (9)
- SHEPHERDS (9)
- WISE MEN (7)
- JOSEPH (6)
- ANGELS (6)
- SIMEON (6)
- DREAM (5)
- MARY (4)
- STAR (4)

(Use the number of letters to find place.)

63. ADVENT ACTION 4

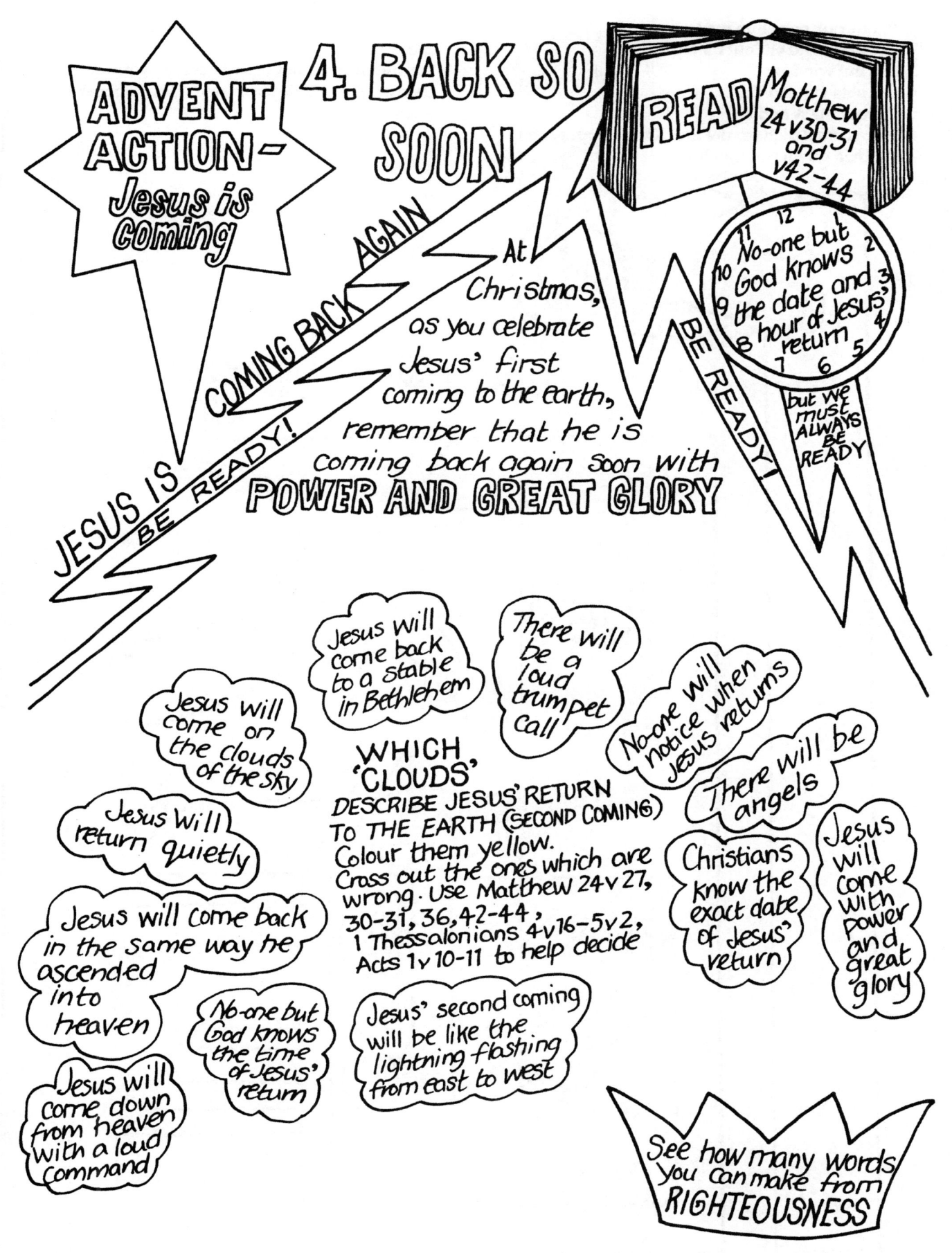

ADVENT ACTION – Jesus is coming

4. BACK SO SOON

READ Matthew 24 v30-31 and v42-44

JESUS IS COMING BACK AGAIN – BE READY!

At Christmas, as you celebrate Jesus' first coming to the earth, remember that he is coming back again soon with **POWER AND GREAT GLORY**

BE READY!

No-one but God knows the date and hour of Jesus' return, but we must ALWAYS BE READY

WHICH 'CLOUDS' DESCRIBE JESUS' RETURN TO THE EARTH (SECOND COMING) Colour them yellow. Cross out the ones which are wrong. Use Matthew 24 v 27, 30-31, 36, 42-44, 1 Thessalonians 4 v16–5 v2, Acts 1 v 10-11 to help decide

- Jesus will come back to a stable in Bethlehem
- There will be a loud trumpet call
- Jesus will come on the clouds of the sky
- No-one will notice when Jesus returns
- Jesus will return quietly
- There will be angels
- Jesus will come back in the same way he ascended into heaven
- Christians know the exact date of Jesus' return
- Jesus will come with power and great glory
- No-one but God knows the time of Jesus' return
- Jesus' second coming will be like the lightning flashing from east to west
- Jesus will come down from heaven with a loud command

See how many words you can make from **RIGHTEOUSNESS**

64. GABRIEL TELLS MARY ABOUT JESUS' BIRTH – ACTION MODEL

1. Photocopy onto thin card.
2. Colour in and cut out both pieces.
3. Cut out window.
4. Cut slits PQ and RS.
5. Pierce dots A and B.
6. From *behind* picture, slot end XY up through slit PQ then down through RS.
7. Line up dot A behind dot B and attach using paper fastener.
8. Start with angel out of sight below window – then pull tab XY down to see Gabriel appear to Mary.

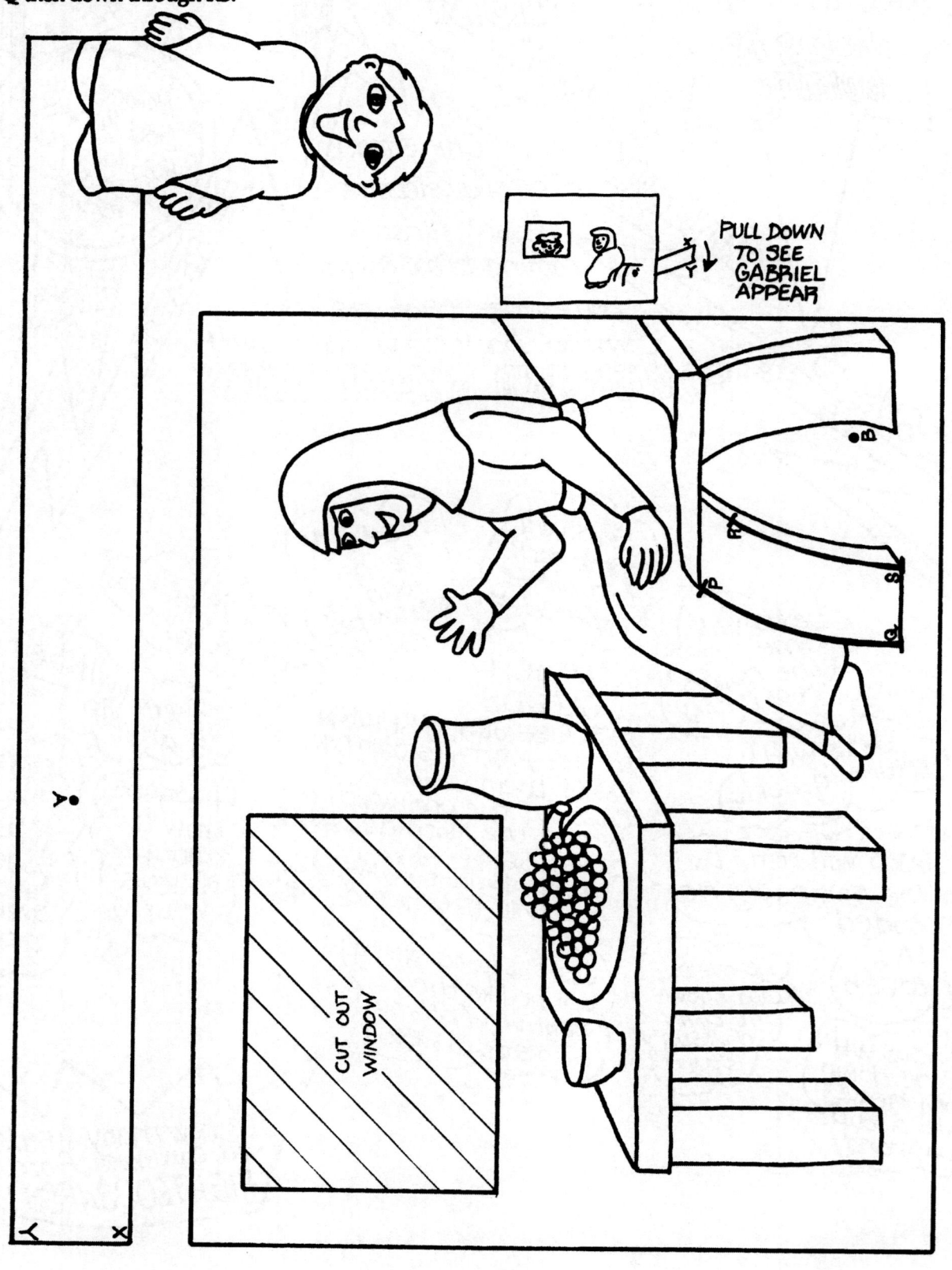

PULL DOWN TO SEE GABRIEL APPEAR

CUT OUT WINDOW

65. FRIEZE – PART ONE

CHRISTMAS ALPHABET FRIEZE

A is for angels who told the shepherds about Jesus' birth.

N is for Nazareth where Mary and Joseph lived.

66. FRIEZE – PART TWO

B is for <u>B</u>ethlehem where Jesus was born.

C is for <u>C</u>hrist which means God's Anointed One.

O is for <u>o</u>xen in the stable where Jesus was born.

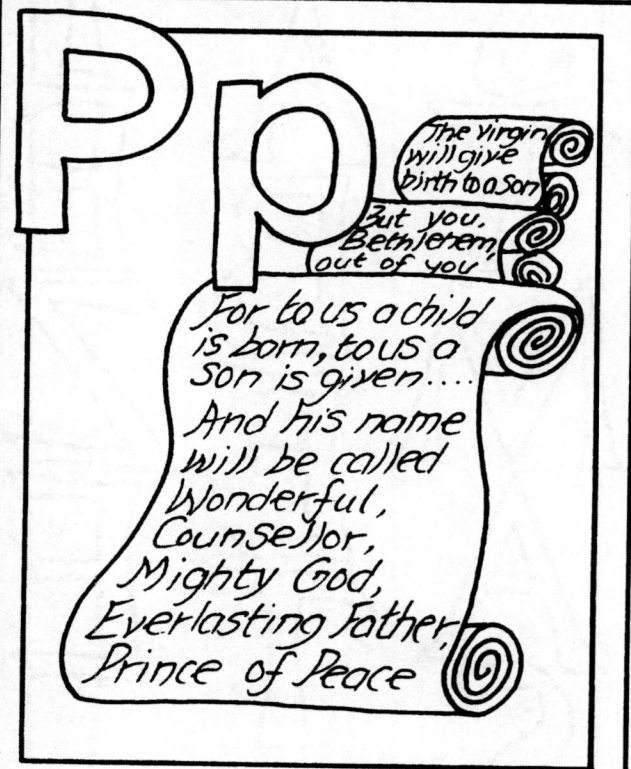

P is for the <u>p</u>romise of Jesus' coming, foretold by the prophets.

The virgin will give birth to a son.

But you, Bethlehem, out of you...

For to us a child is born, to us a son is given.... And his name will be called Wonderful, Counsellor, Mighty God, Everlasting Father, Prince of Peace

67. FRIEZE – PART THREE

D is for the <u>d</u>ream which warned the wise men about Herod.

E is for <u>E</u>mmanuel, God with us.

Q is for <u>q</u>uickly the shepherds hurried to Bethlehem.

R is for no <u>r</u>oom at the inn for Mary and Joseph.

68. FRIEZE – PART FOUR

Ff

F is for frankincense brought to Jesus by the wise men.

Gg

G is for gold, a precious gift given to Jesus by the wise men.

Ss

S is for the star which guided the wise men to Jesus.

Tt

T is for the temple where Simeon and Anna waited for Jesus' coming.

69. FRIEZE – PART FIVE

H is for Herod who was very jealous of the new-born King.

I is for the infant Jesus, taken to Egypt to escape Herod's rage.

U is for Zechariah being unable to speak until John was born.

V is for the Virgin Mary, the mother of Jesus.

70. FRIEZE – PART SIX

J is for Joseph, the husband of Mary.

K is for Jesus, King of Kings.

W is for the wise men who worshipped the baby Jesus.

X is for exciting news of Jesus' birth, told by the angels.

Glory to God in the highest, and on earth peace to men on whom his favour rests

71. FRIEZE – PART SEVEN

L is for the love of God showed in sending Jesus.

M is for myrrh, the third gift brought by the wise men.

Y is for the young child, wrapped in strips of cloth and lying in a manger.

Z is for Zechariah, the father of John the Baptist.

72. BETHLEHEM FOLD-UP CHRISTMAS CARD

1. Photocopy onto thin card – a dark colour, black, blue or purple.
2. Cut out outline.
3. Fold on foldlines.
4. Cut small yellow squares approximately 1 cm x 1 cm out of paper, gummed paper or yellow sticky labels – they do not need to be measured exactly – a slight unevenness will add to the effect. Cut rectangles for the 2 doors.
5. Stick in place on marked dotted spaces to give a 'lighted' window effect on the silhouette of Bethlehem at night.

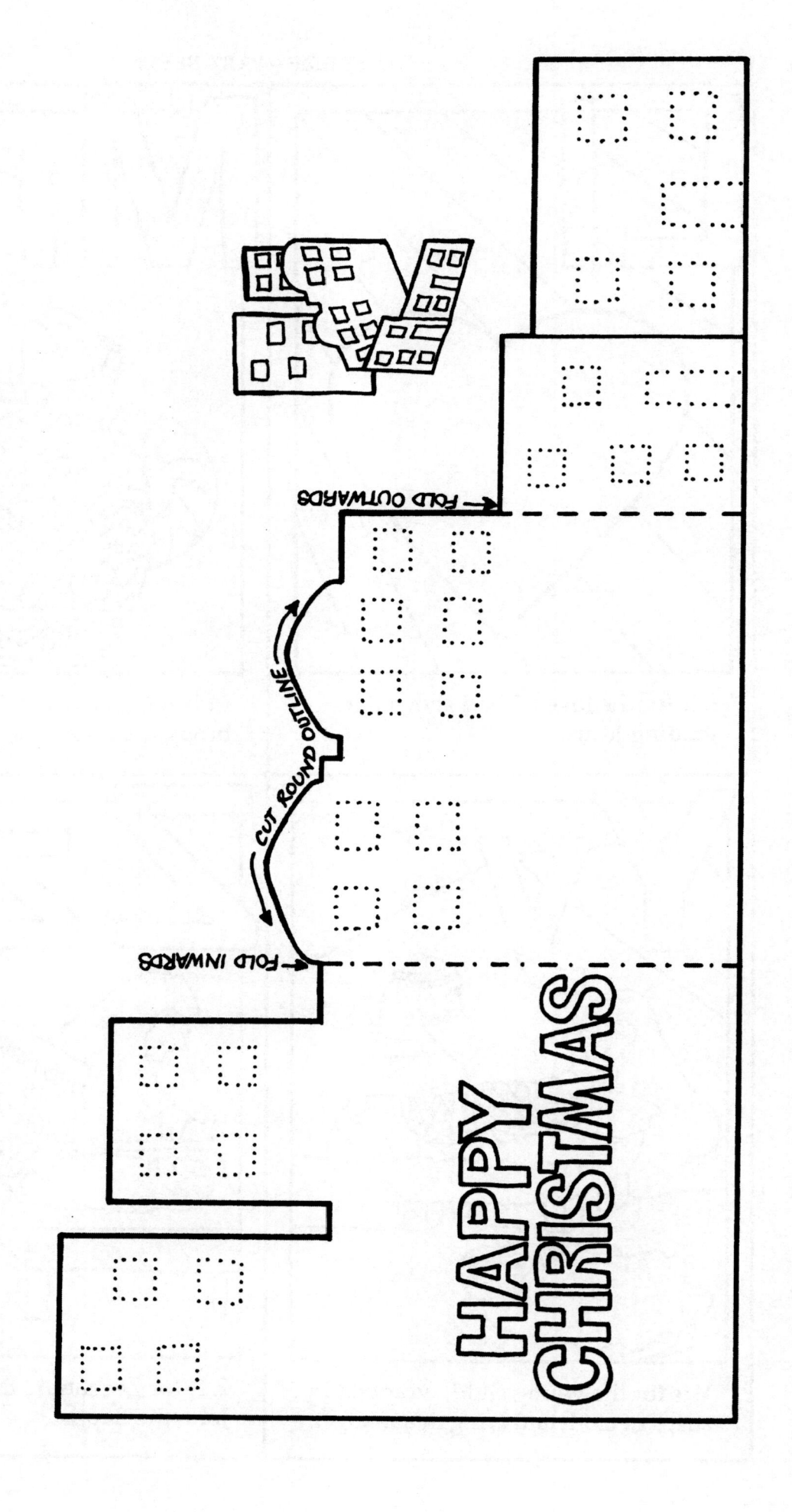

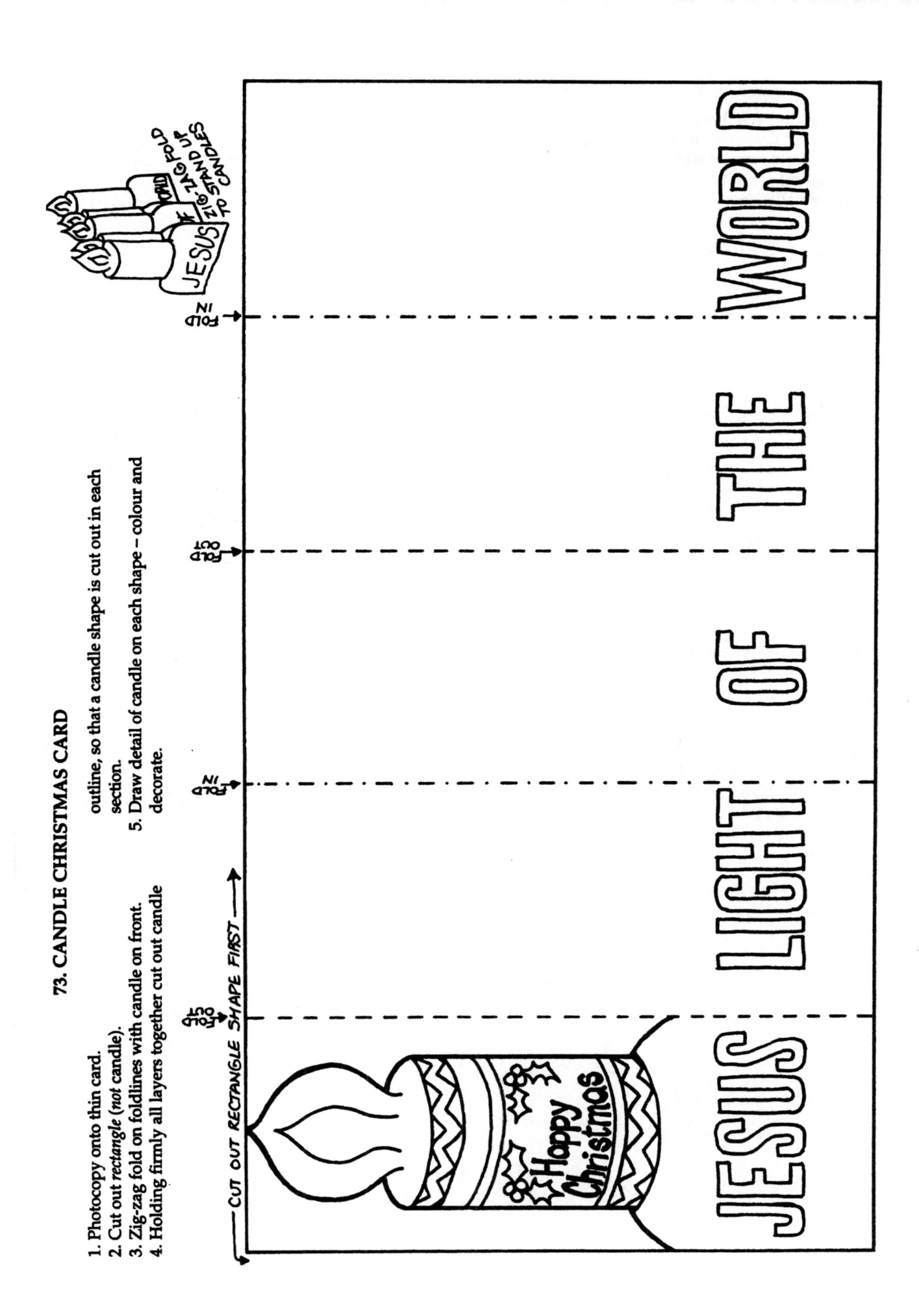

73. CANDLE CHRISTMAS CARD

1. Photocopy onto thin card.
2. Cut out *rectangle* (*not candle*).
3. Zig-zag fold on foldlines with candle on front.
4. Holding firmly all layers together cut out candle outline, so that a candle shape is cut out in each section.
5. Draw detail of candle on each shape – colour and decorate.

JESUS / LIGHT / OF / THE / WORLD

Happy Christmas

74. POP-UP STAR CHRISTMAS CARD

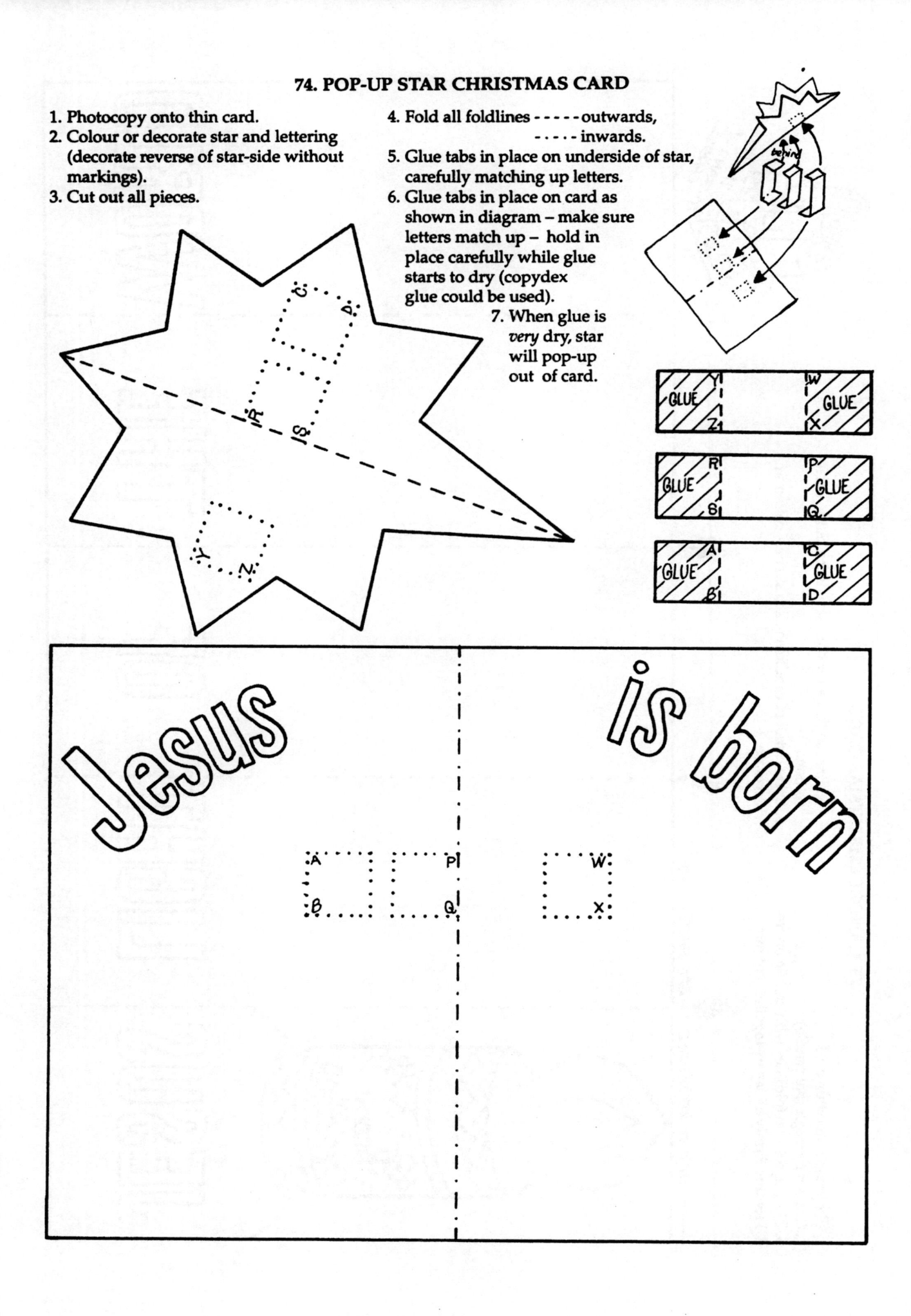

1. Photocopy onto thin card.
2. Colour or decorate star and lettering (decorate reverse of star-side without markings).
3. Cut out all pieces.
4. Fold all foldlines - - - - - outwards,
   - - - - - inwards.
5. Glue tabs in place on underside of star, carefully matching up letters.
6. Glue tabs in place on card as shown in diagram – make sure letters match up – hold in place carefully while glue starts to dry (copydex glue could be used).
7. When glue is *very* dry, star will pop-up out of card.

Jesus is born

75. CHRISTMAS STORY SPINNER – PART ONE

1. Photocopy this and following page onto thin card.
2. Colour and cut out.
3. Cut out two windows in top circle (this page).
4. Pierce holes A and B, then join circles with paper fastener through A then B.
5. Starting at Event 1, turn top circle to go through the events of the Christmas story.

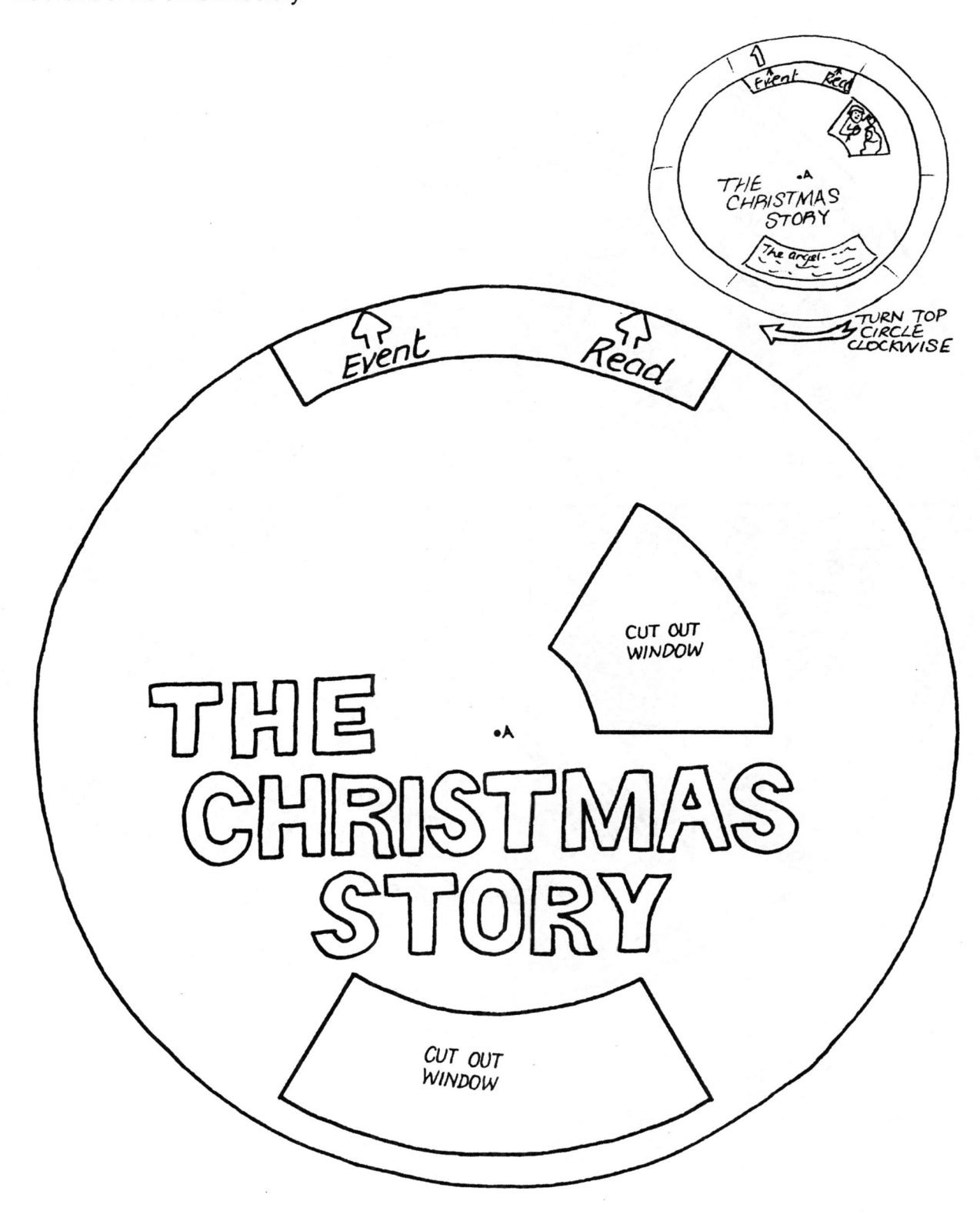

76. CHRISTMAS STORY SPINNER – PART TWO

1. Luke 1 v 26-38 — The angel Gabriel visited Mary to tell her about the coming birth of Jesus.
2. Luke 2 v 1-5 — Mary and Joseph had to go to Bethlehem to register in the Roman census.
3. Luke 2 v 6-7 — Jesus was born in a stable because there was no room for them in the inn.
4. Luke 2 v 8-20 — Shepherds out in the fields saw angels who told them the good news about Jesus' birth.
5. Matthew 2 v 1-12 — Wise men from the east were guided by a star to worship the new-born king.
6. Matthew 2 v 13-18 — Warned by God in a dream, Joseph took Mary and baby Jesus to Egypt to escape from Herod.

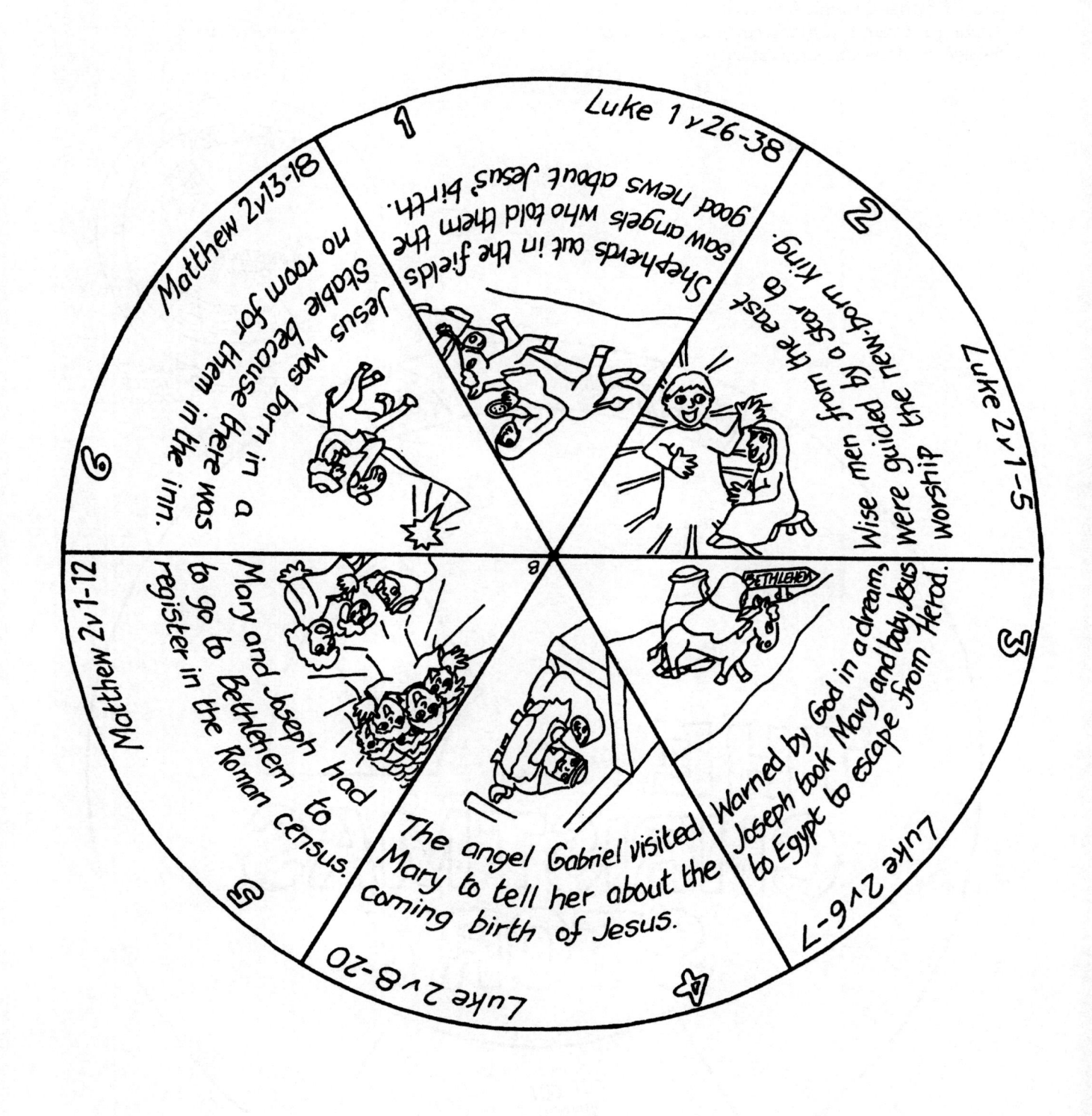

77. CHRISTMAS GIFT BOX

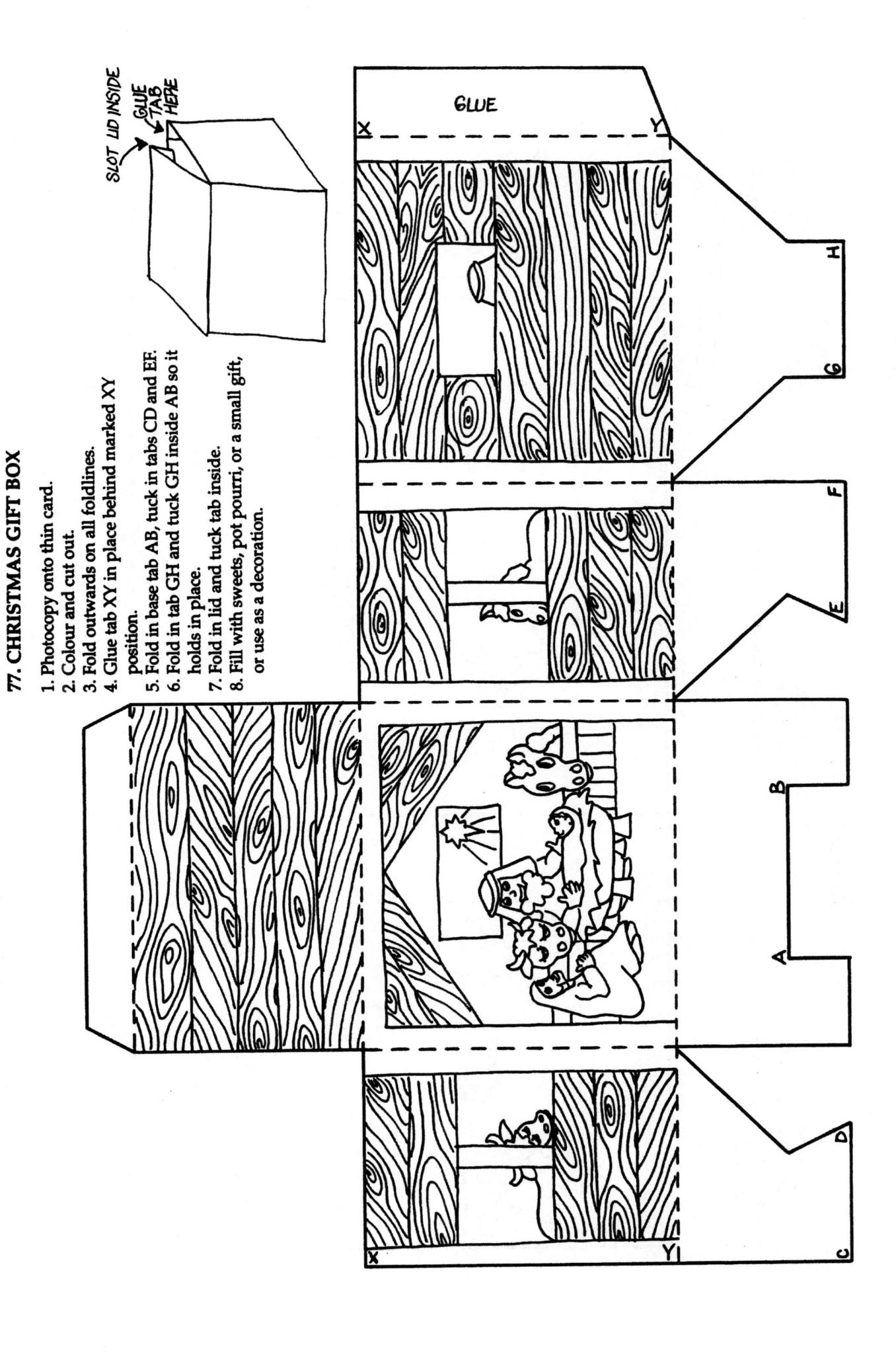

1. Photocopy onto thin card.
2. Colour and cut out.
3. Fold outwards on all foldlines.
4. Glue tab XY in place behind marked XY position.
5. Fold in base tab AB, tuck in tabs CD and EF.
6. Fold in tab GH and tuck GH inside AB so it holds in place.
7. Fold in lid and tuck tab inside.
8. Fill with sweets, pot pourri, or a small gift, or use as a decoration.

78. CHRISTMAS MINI GIFT BAG

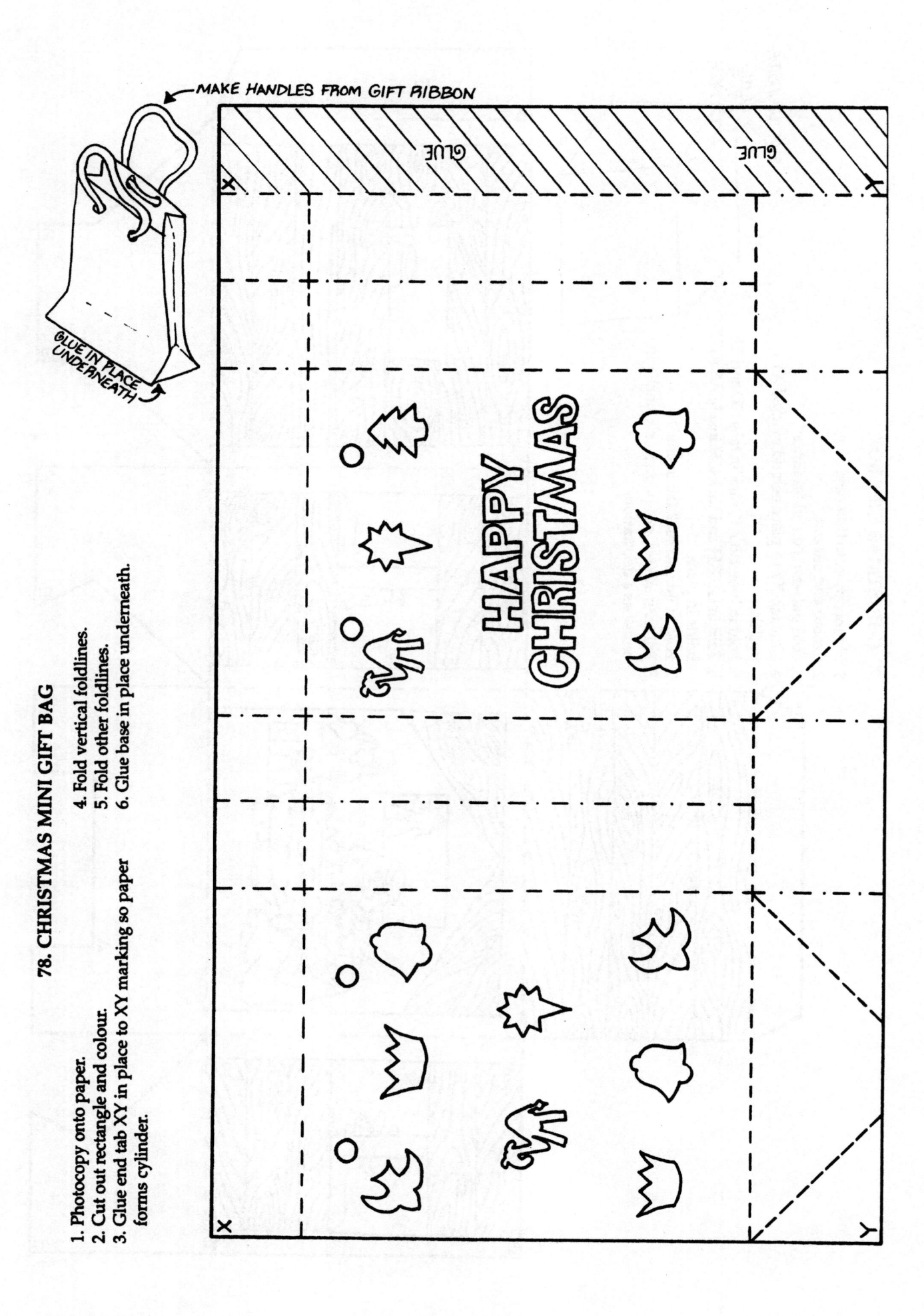

1. Photocopy onto paper.
2. Cut out rectangle and colour.
3. Glue end tab XY in place to XY marking so paper forms cylinder.
4. Fold vertical foldlines.
5. Fold other foldlines.
6. Glue base in place underneath.

MAKE HANDLES FROM GIFT RIBBON

GLUE IN PLACE UNDERNEATH

GLUE   GLUE

HAPPY CHRISTMAS

79. CHRISTMAS FAN DECORATION

1. Photocopy onto paper.
2. Cut out rectangle and colour.
3. Zig-zag fold on foldlines - - - - outwards
   - - - - - inwards.
4. Hold tightly at base and staple on line AB through all layers.
5. Tie gift ribbon round base.
6. Hang up on wall.

80. CHRISTMAS CROWN MOBILE

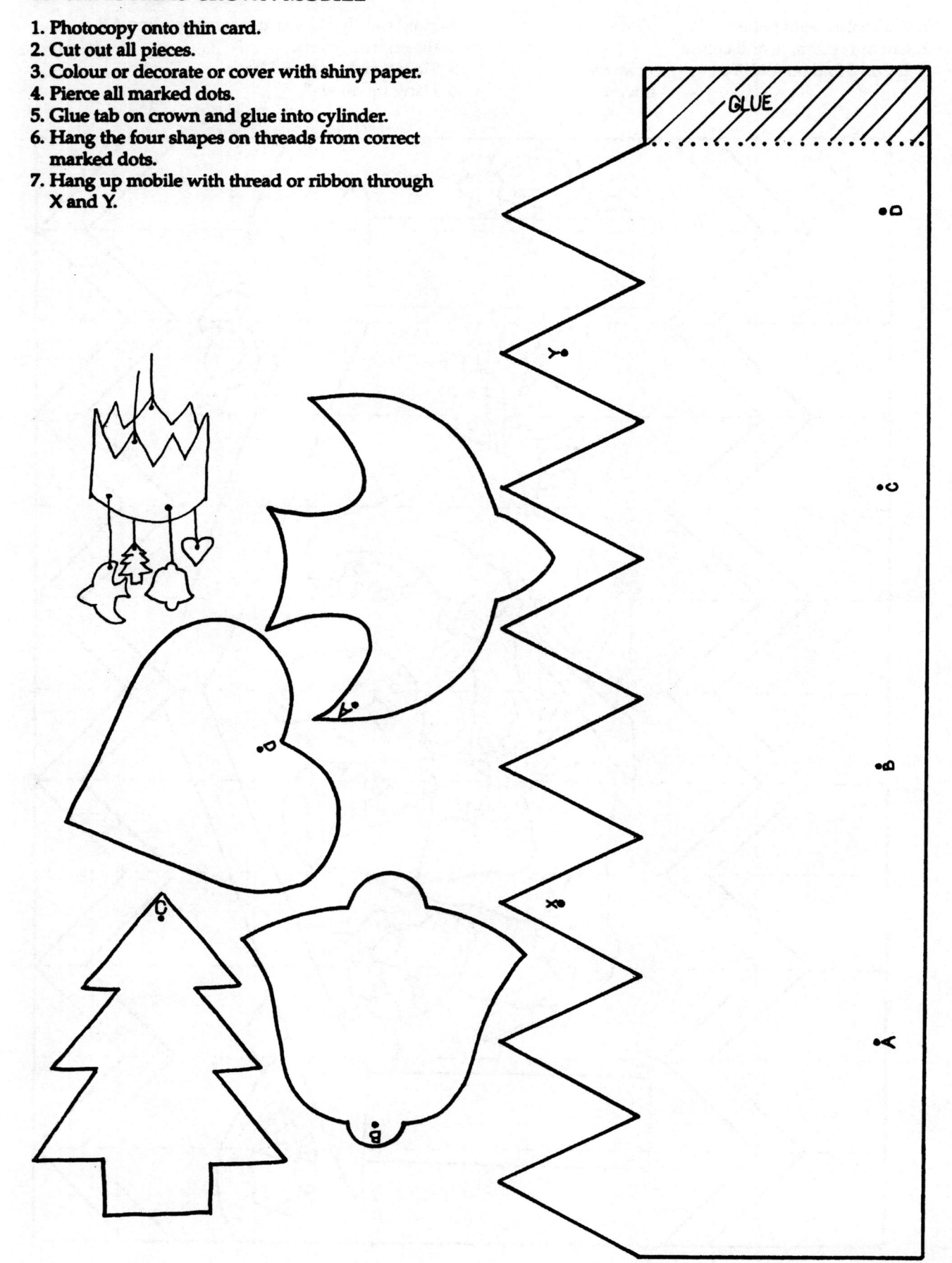

1. Photocopy onto thin card.
2. Cut out all pieces.
3. Colour or decorate or cover with shiny paper.
4. Pierce all marked dots.
5. Glue tab on crown and glue into cylinder.
6. Hang the four shapes on threads from correct marked dots.
7. Hang up mobile with thread or ribbon through X and Y.

81. WISE MEN PRESENT GIFTS – ACTION MODEL

1. Photocopy onto thin card.
2. Cut out and colour in.
3. Cut out window.
4. Pierce dots A and B.
5. Attach circle behind rectangle using a paper fastener through A then B.
6. Line up 'start' arrow, then turn circle clockwise to see wise men present gifts.

(Circle labels: START, gold, fronkincense, myrrh)

TURN CIRCLE TO SEE WISE MEN

On coming to the house, the Magi saw the child, Jesus, with his mother Mary, and they bowed down and worshipped him.

They presented him with gifts of

CUT OUT WINDOW

82. WISE MEN TUBE MODELS – PART ONE

1. Photocopy either – (a) onto card and glue into cylinder
                   or (b) onto paper and glue round a
                          cardboard tube.
2. *Before* gluing, colour in.
3. Repeat with two Kings on following page.
4. Use as a decoration, or tape over base and fill with sweets.

GLUE HERE

83. WISE MEN TUBE MODELS – PART TWO

For instructions see previous page.

GLUE HERE

GLUE HERE

84. CAMEL MASK

1. Photocopy onto thin card.
2. Colour in and cut out.
3. Pierce dots A and B.
4. Cut eyelid slits PQ and RS and ease up slightly folded for eye holes.
5. Attach shirring elastic through holes A and B.
6. Use camel masks to act out the story of the wise men.

85. GOD SPEAKS TO JOSEPH IN DREAMS – ACTION MODEL

1. Photocopy onto thin card.
2. Cut out both pieces and colour.
3. Pierce dots A, and B.
4. Attach circle behind sleeping Joseph using a paper fastener through A then B.
5. Turn circle anticlockwise to see Joseph dreaming.

JOSEPH'S FIRST DREAM – BEFORE JESUS' BIRTH

Take Mary home as your wife – her baby is conceived by the Holy Spirit – she will have a son – you are to call him Jesus, for he will save his people from their sins.

JOSEPH'S 2ND DREAM – AFTER WISE MEN'S VISIT

Get up, take the child and his mother and escape to Egypt – Herod wants to kill the child.

JOSEPH was spoken to by God in dreams 3 times in the Christmas story. The third dream was telling him that Herod was dead and it was safe to go back to Israel.

86. CHRISTMAS STAINED GLASS WINDOW – PART ONE

1. Photocopy onto thin card – a dark colour if possible.
2. Photocopy following page (41) onto *tracing* paper.
3. Cut out windows from card window (this page).
4. Colour pictures (41) using felt pens.
5. On the tracing paper page (41) glue in between dotted lines – glue behind card window, lining up edges.

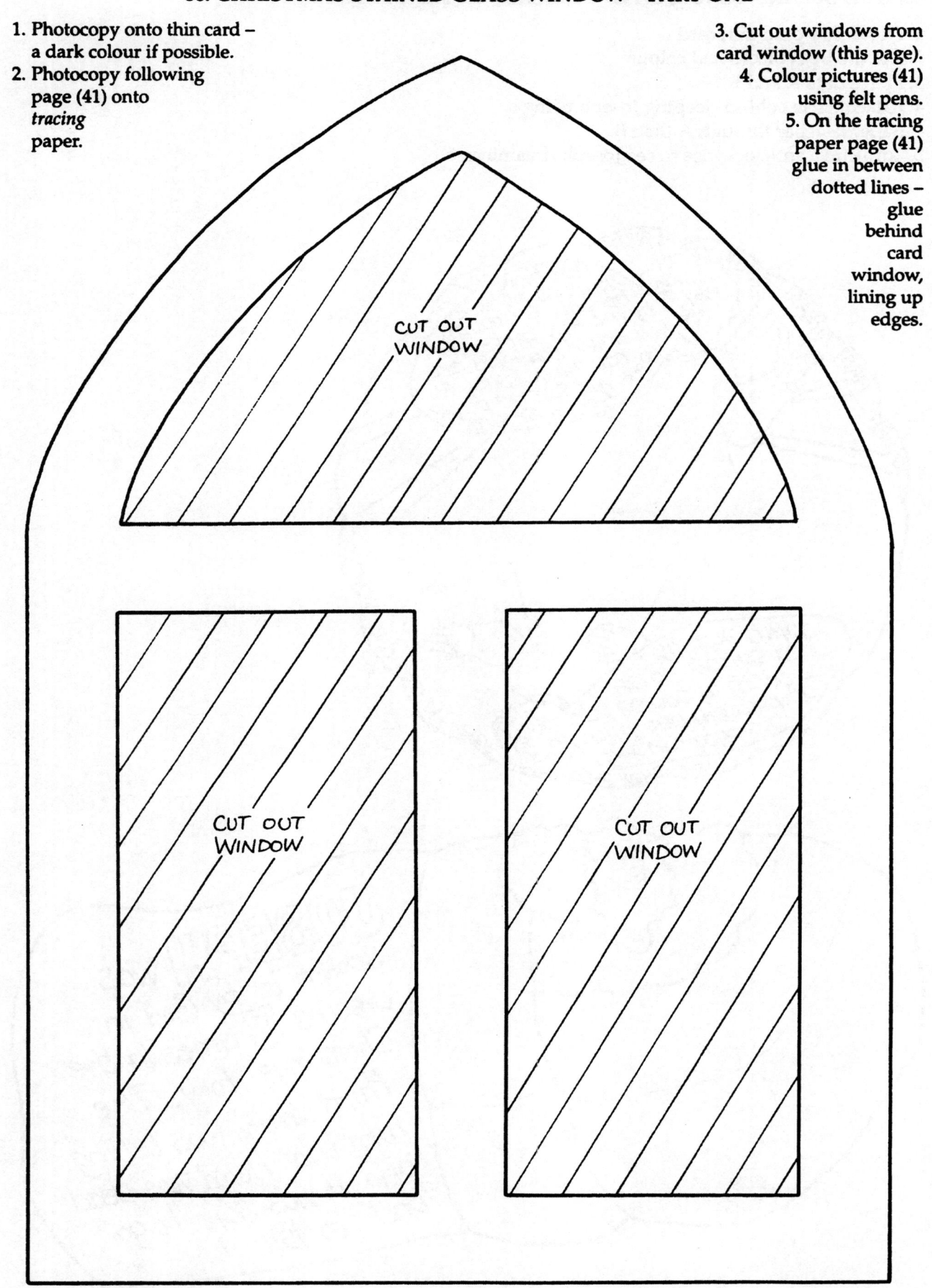

CUT OUT WINDOW

CUT OUT WINDOW

CUT OUT WINDOW

87. CHRISTMAS STAINED GLASS WINDOW – PART TWO

For instructions see previous page.

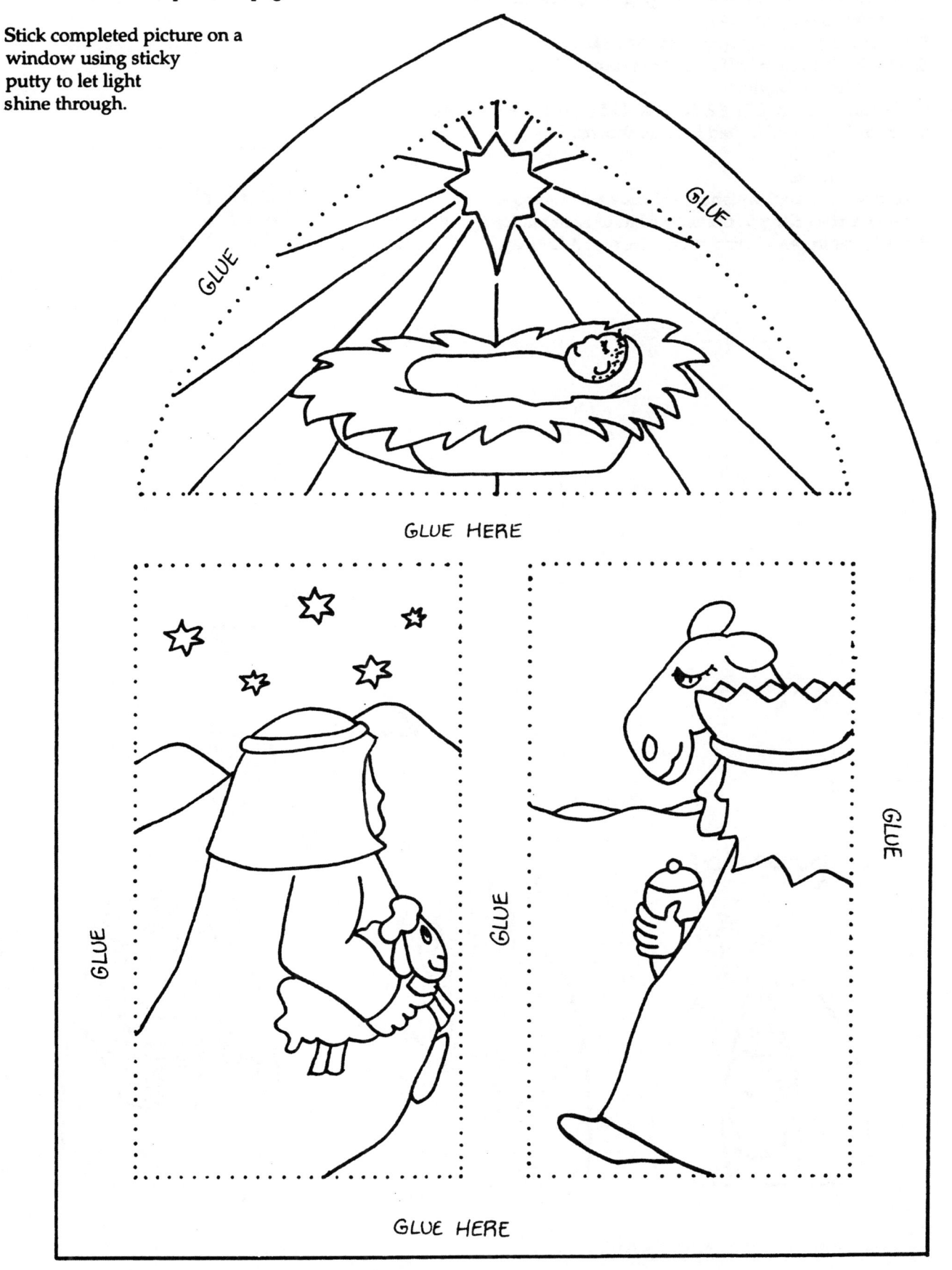

Stick completed picture on a window using sticky putty to let light shine through.

GLUE

GLUE

GLUE HERE

GLUE

GLUE

GLUE HERE

88. POP-UP KINGS CHRISTMAS CARD – PART ONE

1. Photocopy this and following page (43) onto thin card.
2. Cut round rectangle (43).
3. Colour and cut out figures and star (42).
4. Fold base piece in half first along central line, then open flat again.
5. Cut six slits AB, CD, EF, GH, JK, LM on solid black lines.
6. Carefully fold all dotted lines as shown
   - - - - outwards
   - - - - - inwards
   so that 3 rectangles stand out from card base as shown.
7. Glue correct King figure onto front of each marked position.
8. Stick star in place using sticky fixer for 3-D effect.

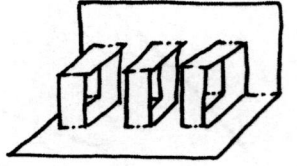

89. POP-UP KINGS CHRISTMAS CARD – PART TWO

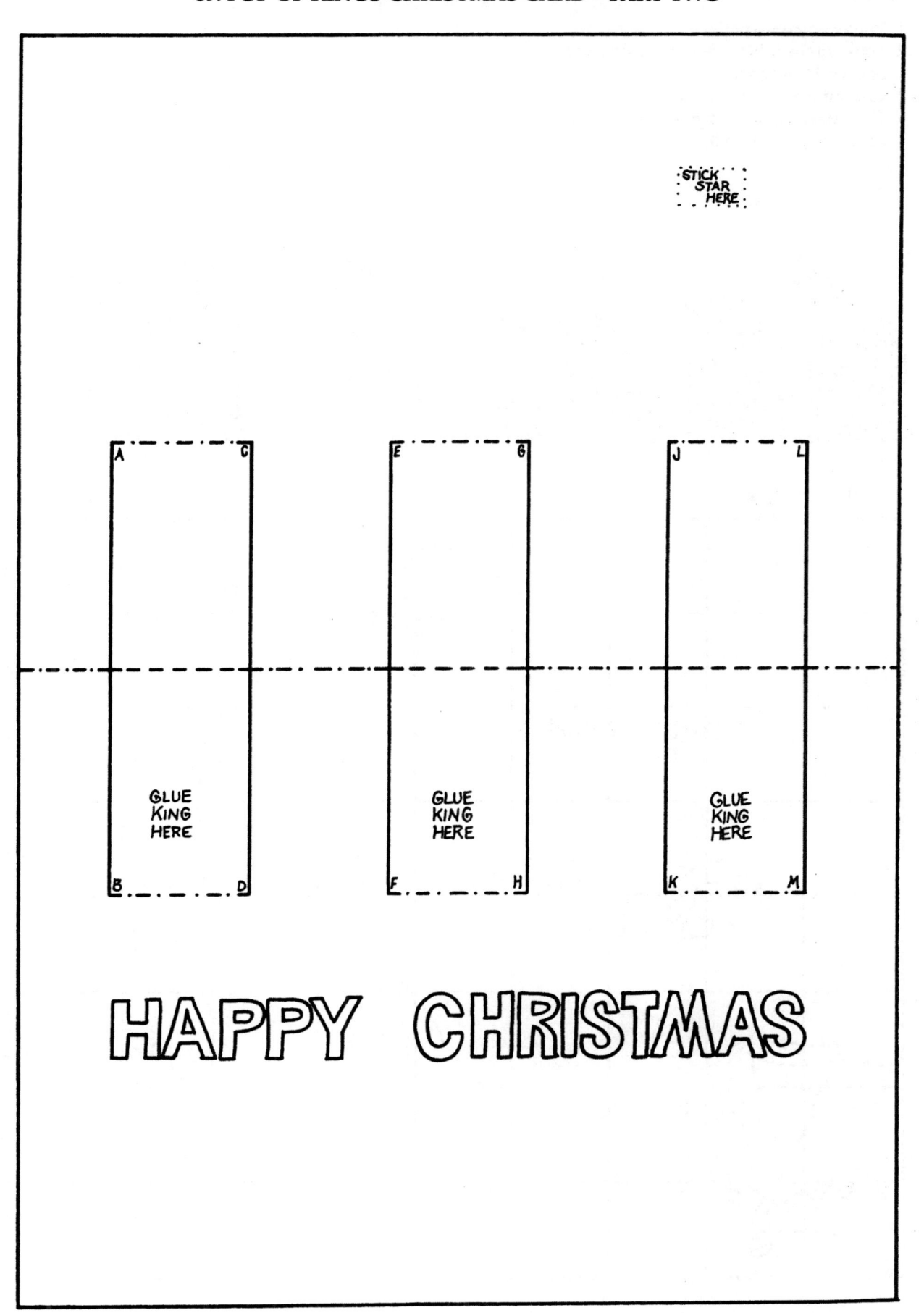

STICK STAR HERE

A C　　E G　　J L

GLUE KING HERE　　GLUE KING HERE　　GLUE KING HERE

B D　　F H　　K M

HAPPY CHRISTMAS

90. CHRISTMAS STORY MAP PUZZLE

1. Photocopy onto paper.
2. Look up the Bible reference to find part of Christmas Story.
3. Cut out the 7 small squares.
4. Glue small squares in position on map according to their map reference.

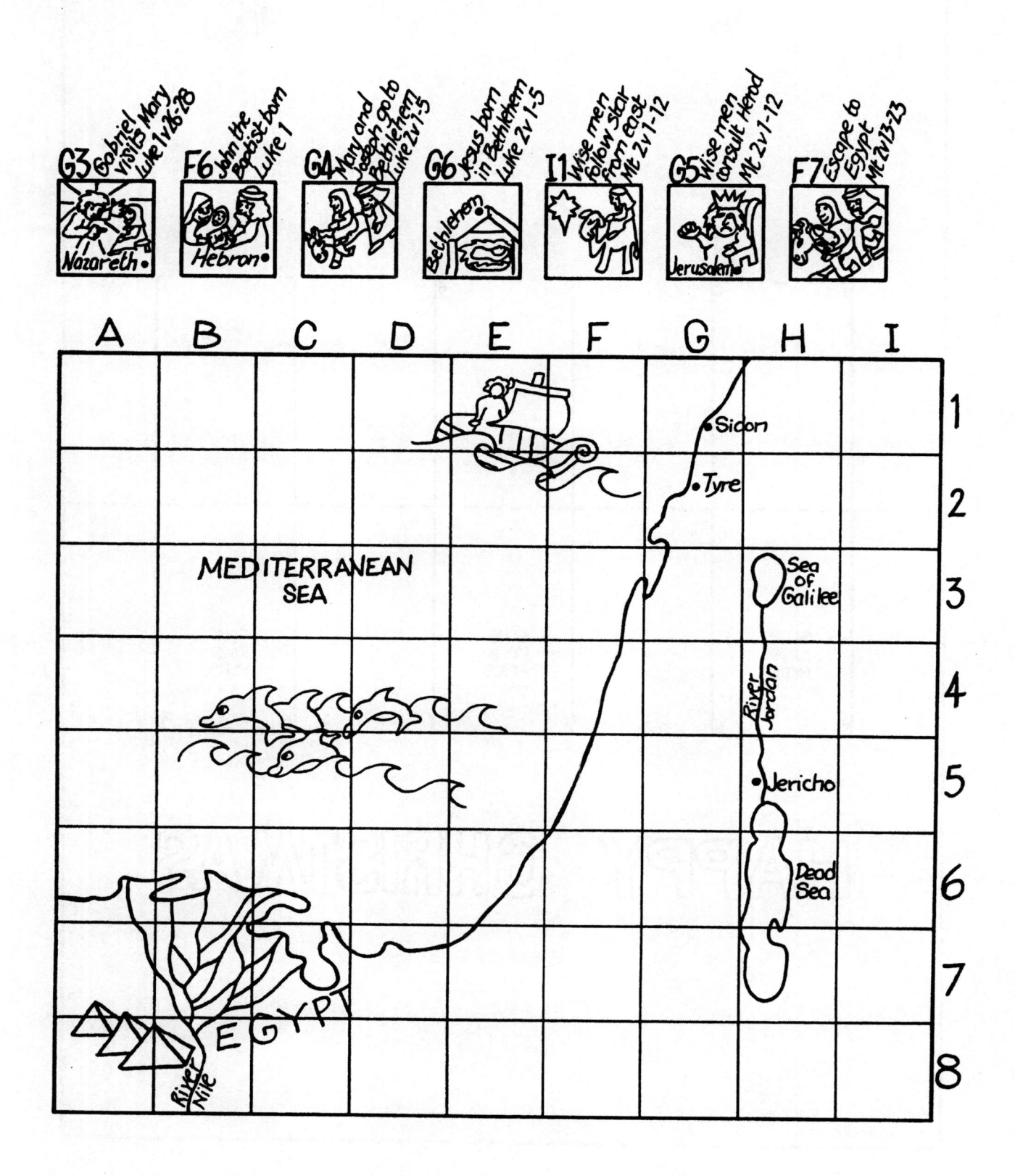

- **G3** Gabriel visits Mary Luke 1 v 26-28 — Nazareth
- **F6** John the Baptist born Luke 1 — Hebron
- **G4** Mary and Joseph go to Bethlehem Luke 2 v 1-5
- **G6** Jesus born in Bethlehem Luke 2 v 1-5
- **I1** Wise men follow star from east Mt 2 v 1-12
- **G5** Wise men consult Herod Mt 2 v 1-12 — Jerusalem
- **F7** Escape to Egypt Mt 2 v 13-23

91. CHRISTMAS QUIZ-SEARCH

From the Christmas story, find the following in the Wordsquare:
(Look in Matthew 1:18 – 2:23 and Luke 1:5 – 2:40 if you are stuck)

THREE people whose names begin with the letter 'J'

THREE towns

TWO mothers whose babies were foretold by angels

THREE presents given to Jesus

TWO people waiting in the temple for Jesus' coming

TWO groups of people who visited baby Jesus

A bad king

Someone who couldn't speak for a while

A sign in the sky

The Roman Emperor

A humble bed for a baby

No room here

Wise men came from here

Building where Jesus was born

Wise men warned in this

Mary and Joseph fled here with Jesus

M	Z	M	E	H	E	L	H	T	E	B	C	I	O	R
E	E	F	J	E	K	R	J	A	S	I	A	N	N	G
A	L	Z	F	R	A	N	K	I	N	C	E	N	S	E
S	I	M	E	O	N	Y	G	J	M	N	S	J	Z	L
T	O	A	J	D	M	N	O	E	R	U	A	E	G	I
E	J	N	S	G	N	S	L	S	Z	M	R	Z	U	Z
M	A	G	I	F	E	A	D	U	M	A	A	T	T	A
A	K	E	L	P	S	R	Z	S	Y	S	U	R	P	B
E	G	R	H	U	V	A	D	A	R	E	G	F	Y	E
R	H	B	R	C	I	D	X	Z	R	J	U	Y	G	T
D	Z	E	C	H	A	R	I	A	H	E	S	B	E	H
O	J	O	H	N	A	P	E	L	B	A	T	S	L	R
M	A	N	S	T	S	A	H	Y	C	G	U	H	V	D
I	Z	T	S	D	R	E	H	P	E	H	S	W	E	J

92. CHRISTMAS STORY – FIND THE ORDER PUZZLE

1. Photocopy onto thin card.
2. Colour and cut out the 8 cards.
3. See if you can put them in the order in which they happened.
4. You can make a 'mini frieze' by gluing them onto a long, narrow strip of card or stiff paper.

In Bethlehem, there is no room for them at the inn.

Mary and Joseph have to take baby Jesus to Egypt to escape Herod's jealous rage.

The angel Gabriel visits Mary to tell her about Jesus' birth.

Angels tell shepherds in the fields the good news about Jesus' birth.

Jesus is born in a stable, wrapped in strips of cloth, and placed in a manger.

Led by a star, wise men travel from the east to find the new-born King.

Wise men worship Jesus and present gifts of gold, frankincense and myrrh.

Mary and Joseph travel from Nazareth to Bethlehem for the Roman census.